T0039248

# SCARS
## *to*
# STARS

*Reflections of a Dubious Daughter*

CLAUDINE K. SEIBERT

**BALBOA**
PRESS

A DIVISION OF HAY HOUSE

Copyright © 2016 Claudine K. Seibert.

All rights reserved. No part of this book may be used or reproduced by any means, graphic, electronic, or mechanical, including photocopying, recording, taping or by any information storage retrieval system without the written permission of the author except in the case of brief quotations embodied in critical articles and reviews.

Balboa Press books may be ordered through booksellers or by contacting:

Balboa Press
A Division of Hay House
1663 Liberty Drive
Bloomington, IN 47403
www.balboapress.com
1 (877) 407-4847

Because of the dynamic nature of the Internet, any web addresses or links contained in this book may have changed since publication and may no longer be valid. The views expressed in this work are solely those of the author and do not necessarily reflect the views of the publisher, and the publisher hereby disclaims any responsibility for them.

The author of this book does not dispense medical advice or prescribe the use of any technique as a form of treatment for physical, emotional, or medical problems without the advice of a physician, either directly or indirectly. The intent of the author is only to offer information of a general nature to help you in your quest for emotional and spiritual well-being. In the event you use any of the information in this book for yourself, which is your constitutional right, the author and the publisher assume no responsibility for your actions.

Any people depicted in stock imagery provided by Thinkstock are models,
and such images are being used for illustrative purposes only.
Certain stock imagery © Thinkstock.

Print information available on the last page.

ISBN: 978-1-5043-4769-3 (sc)
ISBN: 978-1-5043-4848-5 (e)

Balboa Press rev. date: 4/15/2016

# Contents

I dedicate **SCARS TO STARS** to David Sedaris. His brilliant books helped me persevere through the darkest of times. Thank you to Claude, Claudine, Theresa, Muffy, and my forever friends. I want to acknowledge the incomparable Michael Christian for his guidance.

# Introduction

## "You're never dealt a hand that you can't play."

When you're a little kid, you rarely think about taking care of your parents. Even when mom and dad do less than a stellar job, you still look up to them and figure that it's their duty to watch over you. If a single mother or father, relatives, or foster parents raise you, a young imagination doesn't dwell upon what it would be like to have the caretaking roles reversed. Heck, you can be middle-aged and still find it difficult to bear the reality that your folks have reached the stage that they can't fend for themselves anymore.

It's akin to coming down with a bad cold. You're always in a state of denial when the slight achiness begins. Your nose starts running intermittently and the coughing starts. At that viral point, most people continue to blame their blossoming illness on an uncomfortable desk chair or cat dander before they admit that they've been stricken with another case of the sniffles. And so it goes with observing mom and pop getting older, weaker, more forgetful, sickly, and in many cases, totally helpless. You ask yourself, "How in the world am I going to deal with this incredibly depressing and time consuming situation?"

The first step is to console yourself with the fact that the same scenario has repeated itself since humans inhabited the Earth. If the Neanderthals, ancient Egyptians, and Elizabethans did it, so can you. The belief that no one is ever given a burden that is too heavy to carry is the one thought that kept me going when I parented my folks. I also discovered that the venerable tenet, love never dies, became a solid oak tree that I clung to as the winds of change attempted to sweep me off my feet. Most importantly, whether you are aware of it or not, divine guidance will accompany you every step of the way as you serve your loved ones.

Of course every clan handles the delicate matter of mortality in their own unique fashion. If you have siblings and/or extended family members that are willing to lend a hand, you are fortunate *if* they can control themselves. The energy and expenses can be divided. Sometimes traditions have to be broken due to financial setbacks. Dad and I had to have mom cremated and her ashes dispersed in the Atlantic Ocean instead of the original plan of a regal burial in New York.

If you are single like me, it is technically easier to leave your home, friends, and job because you don't have to relocate your spouse and children. In my particular case, I simply couldn't continue flying back and forth from New York to Florida after a certain juncture. So I moved down south. Either way, when a family member begins to fade and you initiate changes and make important decisions for them, it is vital to remember to delegate responsibilities whenever possible. You need to take care of your emotional, physical, and intellectual well-being. If not, you won't be able to support the infirm in their greatest time of need.

You may get in some practice beforehand. Perhaps your mom will have a radical hysterectomy or your dad will undergo kidney, prostate, hernia, and spinal surgery such as my parents. Maybe an uncle and grandfather will succumb to cancer or both grandmothers will be taken by congestive heart failure like my relations. Naturally, you will attend wakes and funerals of friends, business associates, long lost cousins, and a variety of loved ones during your lifetime. Somehow nothing compares to burying or cremating the woman who brought you into this world and the man who adored her.

It doesn't matter how you deal with it; an emotional toll is extracted from everyone involved including your parents. Visualize being the former head of a household and your fully grown "child" confiscates the car keys. Think of how it feels to lose your independence and recognize that it's essential to depend upon a mobile supply of oxygen, a wheelchair, a walker, or the arm of a caretaker to simply transport yourself across a room. Consider becoming incapable of managing your finances or preparing a modest meal. The other side of the coin is the numerous amount of parents who torture their graying offspring because they don't want to become dependent on anyone, downsize to a more manageable home, go to a hospital for the umpteenth time, or utilize lifesaving medical devices. One of my dad's maddening tricks was depositing crucial medication in his pocket the moment I turned my back. How about the parent who continues to smoke like a chimney when his lungs are so destroyed by emphysema that getting out of a chair is a chore? Patience is truly a virtue.

Fast forward; picture watching a cherished family member succumb before your very eyes. How do you deal with conflicting feelings? Yes, it will be a complicated task to carry on without that treasured person. Yet, there is often a distinct sense of relief that a battle has ended. Take heart in the fact that the day will come when you lie down to go to sleep and your pillow won't be dampened with tears. You *can* come to the realization that you were actually fortunate to have been a part of the completion of a life cycle. The rewards are countless. You *will* continue to thrive as guardians, guides, and innumerable instances of divine intervention present themselves to you on a daily basis.

When someone dear has moved on to the next plane, embrace your grief and face it head on or it can consume you. I remember breaking down if I glanced at a piece of key lime pie in a restaurant because it was my mother's favorite dessert. Oftentimes I would dissolve in a pool of tears in the supermarket if I glanced at one of dad's favorite soft drinks. The bottom line is, "Who really cares if I cry in public?" There is absolutely nothing to be ashamed about. If I wept in the soup aisle, I always felt a whole lot better by the time I reached the fruits and vegetables section. Suppressing heartfelt emotions would have encumbered the rest of my experiences that day. Think of what happens when people repress their feelings all of the time. Physical, mental, and spiritual ailments present themselves.

On the other hand, regret is a dismal and useless emotion which should be sidestepped at all costs. Comb through your memory bank as far back as you can. Decipher which recollections will serve you in the future and disregard the rest. Share your history and the knowledge you gained with your pals, kin, acquaintances, and strangers. After your caretaking responsibilities conclude, you have the capability to continue to evolve into a more mature and compassionate person. You will look at life in a completely different manner. Trust that you will eventually pick yourself up off the floor and continue living with a fresh set of eyes and a lighter heart. I did.

*SCARS TO STARS* was written as a cathartic exercise after the conclusion of my time as a caregiver for my mother and father, Claude and Claudine Seibert. My most memorable experiences with my distinctive mom and dad, their quirky folks, and the growing pains we experienced from my childhood to their demise are the seeds from which this book sprouted. Lively decades soared by until each hour became a series of intense emotional experiences steeped in frailty. The skills and strategies I employed in caring for my parents and the unconditional assistance I received from loyal buddies, Hospice of Palm Beach County, and total strangers constitute the final segments of *SCARS TO STARS*.

What I lived through with my mother was totally different from the period of time I spent with my father. Hospice helped me to remember that there is no single path for a caregiver and that I was not alone. The Green Team of Hospice became my caregivers too. They taught me that my future depended upon my willingness to heal and a positive outlook. Revisiting my experiences with my family in *SCARS TO STARS* is one of the many ways I learned to cope with their passing, free myself from the past, and recreate a meaningful life.

# Part I: "That will never happen to me."
## Chapter 1

### "There's nothing keeping us here."

Watching my folks fade away was a difficult process. When I thought they couldn't hold on much longer, they'd come up for more air and carry on for another few years. The specters of sickness and dwindling funds continually haunted them. They never had an opportunity to save for a rainy day because they were too busy getting swindled or throwing a party.

On a whim my father decided to move from Connecticut to Florida in spite of my mother's poor health. It was bewildering to hear my parents apprise me of the fact that they were moving over one thousand miles away because, "There's nothing keeping us here." What a confidence building statement for an only child to hear and such a thoughtful gesture to notify me by phone. Not surprisingly, Claude and Claudine's move to Florida wasn't typical by any means. One would assume that older people such as my folks would take a cab or limousine to a New York airport and fly directly into Palm Beach. No, that would be too easy.

Mom detested flying so she convinced dad to drive to Florida. The only way I know how to get there is Interstate 95. However, my mother felt uncomfortable on I-95 because of the "gigantic speeding trucks." She insisted that they take an "alternate route." I was terrified as I visualized the possible scenarios which could evolve as my parents weaved their way through the Deep South. A weepy fond farewell was all I had after their departure for three days. In my mind's eye I saw them bludgeoned in the red clay of Georgia, beaten senseless in North Carolina, and drugged and hogtied in Tallahassee.

Imagine my glee when more than seventy-two hours after our initial goodbyes my slightly tipsy mother called. I could barely hear her because of the sound of roaring engines in the background. I calmly inquired as to their location as I envisioned crazed motorcyclists ready to gang bang her as they forced my drooling father to watch. Somehow, someway, I swear to God, they were in a house of ill repute in South Amboy, New Jersey. My mother explained that they "drove and drove but couldn't figure out how to get to Florida." They finally decided to rest in a motel. There were no closets in their room. The perimeter of the ceiling "was decorated with blinking red cherry lights." The sound of engines was my dad "firing up the Jacuzzi." Mom stated that she "would never sit in that thing because every disease in the world probably lived in there." I envisioned my dad's testicles shriveling with the most severe STD known to mankind.

As we once more said goodbye, ma gave me their latest travel update. They decided to hire an agent to map out their way to Florida. I simply stated that I loved them and prayed for their safety. Sometimes you just have to give up and hope for something a little less than total disaster.

## "How dare you wear falsies!"

Giving the impression of being wealthy and stylish was the basic tenet of my mother's religion. I often wondered if pickling oneself in vodka, partying until dawn on the weekends, and scarring children for life were the principal elements of Catholic dogma. Forget the fact that I was the only one in the family who confessed my sins once a week and attended 9:00 mass on Sundays. My father was a Republican Protestant. He gave mom free reign concerning the divine beings I would worship and where I would be educated. My very spirit was entrusted to a woman who kept a beige plastic Infant Jesus of Prague next to her bed. A flesh colored Johnson's Band-Aid secured a dollar bill that was stuffed in its base. This meager offering was supposedly an inexpensive insurance policy against all incarnations of evil.

Ma delegated the salvation of my soul and psyche to the Dominican and Ursuline nuns. It is a testimony to my stamina that I survived those thirteen long years of parochial instruction after being teased with the prospect of being taught by a lay person in kindergarten. Naturally, I encountered a few genuinely devoted, intelligent, and compassionate women of God during my formative years. However, the vast majority of them needed unlimited amounts of Valium. My second grade teacher looked like a quarterback in drag. My third grade teacher beat the crap out of us. I clearly remember how a large lipped lad named Jimmy made the deadly mistake of positioning one paper upside down in the stack of spelling tests he had collected from his quivering classmates. Sister Frances looked in horror at the misplaced examination and flung all of the quizzes into the air. It was like watching a movie in slow motion. My fellow students and I witnessed her throw Jimmy to the floor and repeatedly kick him in the stomach as the exams floated to the ground. She didn't even perspire after her brutal exertion. We thought our victimized comrade had perished from a punctured colon. A bleary-eyed lad eventually arose, carefully collected the papers again, and gingerly handed them into the claws of Satan's sibling.

The entire class damn near died on our first day in fourth grade. Over the summer Sister Frances had been reassigned to our classroom. Spending two years in a state penitentiary would have been less stressful and dangerous. Physical and psychological abuse often went hand in hand in elementary school. Presently I write in a clear and neat cursive. It's amazing that I dare pick up a pen at all. During that infamous time another highly strung nun customarily ordered us to the blackboard to compose sentences for her to dissect and condemn. For some reason the slant of my handwriting displeased her. This onerous fact was brought to my attention by a backhanded slap to the face. My teacher's gold marriage band to God slammed into my braces with such force that the inside of my mouth was damaged for days. This was a safe and holy environment second to none.

When we weren't being beaten, we were encouraged to choose a book from our classroom library which consisted of about fifty selections from the same publisher. Every piece of literature was the biography of a saint. My classmates and I often bruised one another in an effort to get to these sordid tales of rape, torture, execution, deceit, debauchery, and miraculous conception.

The entire female population of my school looked forward to the annual talent show. Creativity and an aptitude for music, song, and dance were never displayed. We were forced to stand like soldiers on bleachers and sing religious and patriotic tunes which our instructor compelled us to learn for months on end. What was the name of our guide into a world of humdrum harmonies from hell? No joke: Mrs. Huntune. Nonetheless, we were overjoyed because we were allowed to wear civilian clothes on this special day. For seven blissful hours we ditched our standard uniform of brown oxfords, navy knee-high socks, azure jumpers, matching boleros, white short sleeved polyester shirts with Peter Pan collars, and monogrammed felt beanies. Ma took me to a fashionable store in honor of this momentous event. We were pleased and proud of how I looked in my brand new dark blue hip hugger skirt which boasted a tasteful pattern of tiny daisies, a white poor boy top, and Pappagallo flats.

I was confused as to why I was ordered to the principal's office on this important day. Perplexity turned into apprehension when the nun who escorted me locked the door behind her. Suddenly, both women rushed at me and began pulling up my shirt. The head honcho screamed accusations pertaining to falsies. Unfortunately, I was unfamiliar with the term. Shortly thereafter, I got the picture and hysterically retorted, "My mother is big too!" I was led to the nuns' lunchroom to await my fate. A male classmate was ordered to walk to town and purchase an extra large, white, man tailored shirt for me to wear during my grade's performance. This baggy garment hung well below my knees. I was humiliated to say the least. It's amazing that I didn't develop a neurosis about my feminine curves.

It is hard to believe but I was actually embarrassed and frightened to tell my mother about those mastrophobic nuns. I let the cat out of the bag about thirty years later when mom and I were reminiscing about the old days. She became incensed and stated that her dear friend, the monsignor, would have shipped those psychotic nuns to Antarctica. I sighed and recalled that I would have given my front teeth to attend Bronxville's public elementary and high schools. I probably would have been a pregnant drug addict by the age of twelve if I had gotten my way.

# "My medicines are behind the Virgin Mary."

Mother suffered from allergies from the time she was a little girl. The register of allergens was lengthy. Dog hair, cat dander, dust, grass, flowers, trees, pollen, and mold were at the top of the list. Like many women, ma wanted to be thinner even though her Botticellian figure made men swoon. Doctors told her that she had an underactive thyroid. Mom also had trouble sleeping sometimes. Therefore, endless amounts of prescriptions and over-the-counter remedies for hay fever, weight loss, insomnia, tension, bronchitis, arthritis, back pain, a nervous stomach, headaches, and hangovers were piled sky high in the kitchen, bathrooms, and master bedroom. Along with these various medications, there were half empty canisters of carcinogenic hair spray, make-up, and the usual products and toiletries females purchase. These numerous items made her spacious medicine cabinets, drawers, and night stand look like a well-stocked pharmacy had exploded. Even the pills had pills.

At the moment of my birth, the obstetrician loudly proclaimed that I was also stricken with formidable allergies. Colorful antihistamines, eye and nose drops, cough syrups, and weekly injections in both arms were prescribed. I had asthma, a hideous barking cough, red eyes, a runny nose, and painful ear infections until I was about twelve years old. When I worshipped in church the echo of my hacking sounded like a wounded hound dog was cowering in a pew. In my elementary classrooms I had a hefty supply of pills, powerful cough suppressants, and a giant spoon stashed behind the three foot high ceramic statue of the Virgin Mary. Any time I felt a tickle in my throat I sashayed up to our Blessed Mother and took a hit of either a wicked tasting clear cough syrup or a revolting tonic that was the color of sludge. Which liquid medicine I downed was left to my discretion. I never bothered with the spoon. It was a hassle to keep it clean and it stuck to the wooden shelf that supported the Mother of God.

On top of all that crap, I had to have an injection in my upper arms each week. My biceps were so tender, swollen, reddened, and actually warm to the touch that I was absolutely miserable for at least two days. Mother created slings out of her vast collection of large and colorful silk scarves to support my aching limbs. Every few years I was tested to see if I had developed any more allergies or if I had been miraculously cured of my congenital disorder. I was stripped from the waist up and told to lie face down on a black leather treatment table which was covered with a landing strip of white butcher block paper. A nurse brought in a steel tray with dozens of syringes neatly positioned in rows. She proceeded to scrape my back with each hypodermic needle. How my flayed skin reacted determined the success or failure of my therapy. I prayed that my hypersensitivities would disappear but the results were always the same: Positive for all allergens.

By the time I reached seventh grade, I had lost faith in doctors, the clergy, and my parents' ability to make prudent decisions. Ma's unwavering belief in the medical profession was frightening. A second opinion was considered an insult to our family physicians. One day I mustered up the courage to tell mom and her army of doctors to go to Hades with all of their hideously flavored medications and painful remedies. I never experienced any symptoms of allergies after that blow up. I ask you now, "What the hell was that all about? Did my parents have their life savings invested in Pfizer stocks?"

The only side effect from liberating me from the bondage of quacks was that I developed a determination to stand up for my rights. The nuns called it "impudence" and gave me a "C" on my report card for "Courtesy and Cooperation." My grandparents referred to me as "bold." My folks dubbed me "a goddamn pain in the ass." Mother and I started to battle. Sometimes a breakfast plate or a butter knife flew in my direction as I headed for the school bus. We were an equal match with regard to physical strength. When we were really angry, mom and I grabbed each other's upper limbs, squeezed as hard as we could, stared into one another's eyes, and cursed like drunken sailors. We both tired of this particular brand of standoff rather quickly. Yet, it released some of our negative energy and we went our separate ways. Dad always knew when we engaged in a contemptible deadlock because ma had navy blue fingerprints on her milky white skin. She always bruised rather easily.

My mother possessed the heart of a fighter even though she was the epitome of femininity. She could thank her dad's Irish blood and her mom's German heritage for that character trait. Steadfastness served her well in the long run. Little did she know how vigorously her mettle would be tested in the decades to come.

# "Where's my chocolate and tequila?"

Mother advised me since kindergarten that I would never have to go to school on my birthday. It didn't matter how heartily anyone in an administrative position objected to her nonconformist belief. Mom just couldn't see why I would have "to work on such an important day." Her policy concerning truancy was incredibly open-minded which startled me at first. Ma also allowed me to skip a day of school when I wasn't ill if I promised I would never play hooky or lie to her about being sick. I never abused the privilege and took advantage of her generous offer a few times a year.

I faithfully observed my personal annual holiday throughout high school and college. When I was employed at my first job, I naturally stayed home on my birthday. Mom had ingrained in me that it was my inalienable right to do whatever I pleased on May 25th. My jaw dropped when my boss called and gave me a no-nonsense reality check. I wised up after that down-to-earth discussion and took my private holy day off its pedestal.

As the years passed, I conducted comparative studies as to how other families handled traditional celebrations and day-to-day problems. I found that Claude and Claudine's solutions to difficulties often caused more dilemmas. Their versions of national holidays were also clearly distinguishable from other households. My parents' interpretation of Easter amused me to no end. As a child I awakened to a thumping sound on the carpet outside my closed bedroom door. I sprang to my feet, flung open the entrance to my darkened cave, and chuckled with delight as I followed a trail of real carrots down the hallway and a flight of stairs. There were numerous orange paths which led to beautiful bulging baskets behind carnation colored satin curtains, a huge potted plant, a stately carved wooden bar, and a lilac velvet settee. My mother and father prepared splendid caramel colored wicker baskets with pink satin bows which were filled with artificial green grass and vast assortments of chocolate bunnies, jelly beans, marshmallow chicks, and colorful eggs.

As I got older, I brought friends home to celebrate Easter Sunday. Mom and dad created delightful baskets for all of us. When I drove up to the house cronies gasped with glee and leapt from the car. We giggled like large children as we gathered armloads of carrot trails as green bushy leaves tickled our arms. My folks waited at the front door with open arms, huge grins, and chilled cocktails. They gently supervised the search by pointing in the general direction of our respective treasures. My basket was special and drew sighs of admiration from my buddies. Naturally, it was the largest and contained what appeared to be a small candy store. The crowning glory of my Easter treat was a gigantic chocolate bunny, my yearly Allstate car insurance statement paid in full, a box of margarita mix, and a bottle of tequila. This marvelous tradition continued until I was well into my forties. The Easter Bunny must have been proud of Claude and Claudine's endeavors.

Mom actually prepared a tasty leg of lamb for dinner at Easter but was intoxicated by the time she had to make the gravy. Ma always sat nearby the cooking appendage and ordered dad to make the sauce to her specifications. I still wonder who taught my mother to save old refrigerated bottles of Heinz ketchup, fill them with hot water, and shake them vigorously. That hideous solution was the base of her liquid topping for potatoes, vegetables, and meat. Perhaps ma's gravy was delicious. I really shouldn't pass judgment because it never came near my taste buds. She also made a scrumptious lamb stew from the leftovers. I looked forward to her cooking on two nights out of the entire year.

Mom had a tight schedule during the week. It was next to impossible to fit in tidying up the refrigerator after a holiday bash between games of bridge, shopping, and attending parties. One evening a few weeks after Easter, I brought a small crowd of hungry and thirsty friends home with me. I figured we'd pile into the kitchen and grab a few snacks and some beverages. Everyone gasped in horror as they viewed the rancid remains of a large leg of lamb swimming in caramel colored gel. This culinary atrocity was resting in a large black roasting pan on top of the stove. My best guess is that mother had run out of room in the fridge and planned to clean up that evil mess in the morning. To make matters worse, she had written a note and propped it up on the botulism special. It read, "DEAR LITTLE CLAUDIE, PLEASE DON'T EAT THIS. LOVE, MA." A malnourished cannibal would have passed up this oozing entrée. One by one, we began laughing uncontrollably as we knew the divine Mrs. Seibert all too well.

## "I know you've got a poodle in there."

I begged for a dog for as long as I can remember. I firmly believe that every child, especially one without siblings, deserves the opportunity to experience a fluffy ball of unconditional love. My overly indulgent grandmother attempted to make my wish come true by purchasing the vast majority of tickets for the St. Joseph's Elementary School Puppy Raffle. It was no surprise that I won. However, the mongrel turned out to be a sickly mutt who made such a mess that even I tired of him. His paws also indicated that he would mature into an unwieldy creature resembling a small horse. I was informed that he ended up at "a fine home in the country." I was left alone once again to fantasize about a manageable mammal. Dad instructed me to cease playing upon my older relative's impressionable heart strings with the solemn words, "It just isn't the right time to get a dog. They cause allergies to flare up, you know."

Time passed but my hopes for a cuddly playmate never subsided. Claude and Claudine pursued their vigorous social life and continued to attend various conventions. Momps and Pops, my maternal grandparents, took care of me during my parents' trips. I have to admit that I missed the dynamic duo after a while. A sense of anticipation always built up as I awaited the arrival of their homebound limo in our driveway. One wintry afternoon, I sat with my legs crossed on the cold tile floor of our solarium and stared out of an arched window. From my vantage point I could see what cars approached our home. Finally, a shiny black Cadillac slithered up the driveway and a well-seasoned, red eyed, silver haired chauffeur named Foxy opened the car door for my mother. She looked like a freaking movie star even after a wearisome trip. Mom's gently tussled platinum hair complemented her white mink coat which she snuggled into as she approached the front door of her mini-castle. Her bright blue eyes crinkled with a smile. Anyone could tell she was glad to be home.

I couldn't contain myself any longer. I took off like a bullet and ran through the living room to greet my dazzling mother and handsome father. I threw my arms around her hips to show how much I missed her. I was shattered as she withdrew from my embrace and uttered, "Now be careful, Claudie!" As tears welled up in my eyes she opened her coat to uncover a handful of cream colored fur. It was the tiniest and most adorable toy poodle pup! I was speechless and in a state of disbelief.

Dad explained how they had visited a farm where race horses were bred. The owner ushered my folks into a large room which was unfurnished except for an enormous Oriental rug. My parents were hoping for a refreshing cocktail to cool them from the merciless Floridian sun. They were rather perplexed when the southern gentleman opened a door at the far end of the chamber and out toddled a dozen magnificent toy poodles of different ages. The chap also raised show dogs.

My father knew that poodles did not shed and were a highly intelligent breed. His parents had owned a black standard female named Jasmine. Mom was won over after a few drinks. The problem was hiding the pooch at the hotel and smuggling it onto their train back to New York. My mother's charm took care of the bellboys at their temporary residence. Ma attempted to conceal her new charge from the porter in my parents' sleeping car. The generous attendant informed her that he was neither blind nor stupid and he wouldn't tell a soul that she had hidden a minuscule puppy in a hat box.

Thus began the reign of the Muffy Dynasty. For fifteen years this "loving roundling," as mom would say, brought incredible joy to our family. Pops, my sometimes gruff grandfather, was terribly annoyed that ma had "disregarded her health" by bringing a "wild animal" into his apartment. My grandmother and mother left him and the Muffster in the kitchen to become acquainted. When they returned he hadn't moved an inch. In fact, Pops appeared to be frozen with the heels of his shiny black leather wingtips touching and his toes pointing outwards like some bulging ballerina in a suit. Ma and Momps dissolved in a fit of laughter when they realized that the innocent pup had fallen asleep between my grandpa's feet. Pops didn't wish to disturb the slumber of the newest member of our clan. The Irish giant's harsh opinion of the canine cutie had melted away in a matter of minutes.

Muffy I, II, and III provided us with an abundance of pleasure and cuddles for forty-three years. My parents could never manage to stop using the typically obnoxious moniker for their three generations of poodles. It didn't really matter because no one could imagine my mom having a dog named anything except Muffy. They were a perfect match.

# Chapter 2

## "You're kidding: Claude, Claudine, and Claudine?"

Many people are familiar with famous duos such as Ozzie and Harriet, Burns and Allen, and Blondie and Dagwood. What about Claude and Claudine? Their names are certainly catchy and rather romantic but I'm sure only several hundred bells rang out there. Such appellations deserve a detailed explanation. It's impossible to calculate how many times I heard an incredulous tone after dad introduced our pocket-sized family, "You're kidding: Claude, Claudine, and Claudine?" Our unique tale commenced on the Metro-North railroad line.

My folks met on a blind date at the New Rochelle, New York train station in 1949. Uncle Ted, dad's older sibling, arranged the destined introduction. Ted met my mom at a social gathering and couldn't wait to introduce her to his younger, more handsome brother. My father resembled a youthful Ricky Ricardo and my mother appeared to be a relative of Marilyn Monroe. They were a handsome couple as they sat side by side during the first of many trips to Manhattan.

Claude and Claudine's romance began on a Manhattan bound train.

14

Mom's parents were attracted by dad's wealthy background and promoted their courtship. The attractive twosome was married on June 2, 1951 at St. Joseph's Church in Bronxville, New York. Their union produced moi, another but very different Claudine. My mother often recited her favorite domestic motto, "It's three against the world!" I knew right off those odds were highly unfavorable.

Mom was a flamboyant, alluring, and unconfident woman. She possessed the body of Liz Taylor and the head of a blonde Loretta Young. Men gawked at her and on innumerable occasions followed her home after a shopping expedition or honked on the road seeking her attention. Bizarre myths evolved around my mother's inimitable sense of style and passion for the color pink. Many a Bronxvillian believed she wore nothing but pink, dyed her toy poodle pink, and drove a pink Cadillac. How silly of them; her Cadillac was lavender. As all mothers do, ma imparted words of wisdom which reflected her quirky philosophy on life, "Always smile at homeless people because everyone deserves a smile. Plus, it catches them off guard and gives you an opportunity to run."

She also advised me to say a little prayer every time I heard or saw an emergency vehicle. This compassionate suggestion probably stemmed from the fact that ma lost her older sister in a car accident. My grandmother grieved for seven years and wore nothing but black during her self-imposed mourning period. Grandma also made it perfectly clear throughout her lifetime that she wished my mom had been killed on that deadly night instead of her "beloved Grace."

Whether it was a barbecue, a gala at a country club, or a business event at a convention, in spite of her low self-esteem, mom earned the well-deserved reputation as "the life of the party." She was a sought after guest at bridge luncheons, fashion shows where she often modeled, cocktail parties, dances, and beach bashes. Ma was flirtatious in an innocent way, vivacious, and downright humorous. It was said, "A dead person could have fun in her presence."

My father consistently acknowledged mom's sincere appreciation of fashion. After they married, dad drew a humble salary from his family's financial newspaper business. He often ignored the inevitable consequences of giving my mother money to purchase a dress instead of paying a utility bill. She looked irresistible even in the dimmest light. Many husbands showered their wives with bouquets of flowers or assorted chocolates on special occasions. How dreary. Dad purchased pastel pumps and black patent leather or velvet stilettos to express his adoration. Mother was always thrilled as father kissed her and surrendered her millionth pair of high heels.

After three years of marriage, dad underwent death defying back surgery and twenty-four months of painful rehabilitation. He had to be loaded on a wooden plank into the backseat of a car to travel anywhere because he couldn't sit for a year after the operation. My steadfast father endured this torture only to accompany my devoted mother to weekend parties so she had a reason to smile during the rest of the week. Later in their lives when he'd recovered but still couldn't bend at the waist, dad vacuumed the carpets of our home on his knees before guests arrived for one of their frequent over-the-top celebrations. My parents threw an annual fete to repay friends for the joys they experienced at their revels. In August, oodles of people arrived at our house and partied until dawn. Dad thought it wise to also invite our neighbors and the local police and fire departments so he wouldn't be cited for disturbing the peace. His ploy worked like a charm.

Many of my folks' pals believed my father loved my mother more than life itself. He purchased the largest and most saccharine Hallmark card for her birthday, their anniversary, and every holiday. Dad signed those sentimental declarations of undying devotion, "Your Boy." Mom treasured his tokens of tenderness for more than half a century of marriage. For fifty-four years the wheel of fortune spun in and out of their favor. The old saying, "What doesn't kill you makes you stronger," surely applies to the legacy of Claude, Claudine, and Claudine. The German origin and meaning of our last name, Seibert, is significant. It is composed of the elements *sigi* meaning 'victory' and *berth* meaning 'bright.'

## "It's March and your Christmas tree is still up!"

In the early 1950's, my maternal grandparents, Milton and Theresa Kennedy, purchased my folks' first home for a song. It was a swell wedding gift even though the grounds needed a lot of work as the backyard was a virtual mudslide. Today, this renovated Mediterranean style white stucco villa is still perched on half an acre of land well above street level in the suburbs north of Manhattan. Back in my day, trellises on either side of the modest pool dripped with clusters of lavender wisteria in the spring and summer months. The complementary bumble bees were so large they had landing gear. Ruby colored roses covered the wooden fence between our property and the neighbors. My buddies and I created a club house in a grotto filled with inexpensive, exotic, porcelain birds which mom ingeniously cemented in its crevices. A verdant rolling hill led to the driveway and witnessed countless sledding accidents when it snowed. Ornate plasterwork adorned high ceilings. Hidden terraces, stone circuitous stairways, an imposing picture window, stained glass arched doors, a black wrought iron spiral staircase, an enormous lion-footed bathtub, Italian tile floors, servants' quarters with no servants in them, a tree house that kids and adults loved to play in, and ghosts galore added a mystique to the place that's still hard to beat.

Technically, our former abode is located in Yonkers, New York. However, the post office declared our mailing address as the village of Bronxville, not "da Bronx." Bronxville is one of the most affluent square miles in the United States and the city of Yonkers is most definitely not. Bronxville was a former artists' colony and boasts of well-to-do residents to this day. JFK's family, Jack Paar, Ed McMahon, Brendon Gill, Durward Kirby, the King of Jordan, and other famous and infamous people lived in this lovely area since the 1800's. Ma threatened me on a regular basis, "There will be bloody hell to pay if you ever divulge the fact we live in Yonkers!" We were from "the wrong side of the tracks." This was a dark and deadly secret never to be mentioned in public.

Our unique home was designed by an obscure movie director and custom built in 1918. He described paintings that hung on the walls of any residence as "distasteful." Consequently, glorious scenes of cobalt and sky blues, saffron, ebony, and creamy white tiles were inlaid in deliciously unexpected places. A seven foot by five foot creation of mythical birds greeted visitors as they neared the front door. Urns bursting with wild flowers appeared on the curved walls of the sunroom. A youthful señorita, who carried a basket of blossoms, adorned a garage wall. I often sat in the driver's seat of our car with a bag of groceries on my lap and gaped at her beauty.

Our unique home and its first owners in the 1920's.

A large, circular, shallow pool in the solarium was in a perpetual state of drought. It brimmed with potted flowers during most of the year as mom possessed a green thumb. The only time the faux fountain wasn't filled with impatiens in every shade of pink was from December through March. My mother and St. Joseph's Church purchased their Christmas trees from the same supplier. Our holiday sequoia was stationed in the arid water feature. This tree was so damn big that it took ages to decorate. Mom didn't possess the heart to take it down until the Easter Bunny was ready to come to town. Forget the fact we would have been incinerated if that giant had ignited.

Come the end of March, dad dutifully hired a squadron of cops who were looking to make some extra money. They removed ma's precious ornaments from the tree and stored them away for next season. The men in blue masqueraded as lumberjacks and hauled the last visible evidence of wild Christmas parties to the dump. Another round of festivities was about to begin as Easter approached.

My mother possessed boxes upon boxes of delicate ornaments from the past which had to be repacked and painstakingly placed in the cavernous attic. Colorful frosted glass orbs and delicate crystal decorations might shatter if you breathed too hard. Some had chubby cherubs or joyous holiday scenes delicately painted on their surfaces. There were even miniature hot air balloons. I made endless trips back and forth helping the policemen strip our esteemed tree.

Unfortunately, all those precious embellishments were lost as squirrels and raccoons destroyed them. As time went by and decay on numerous levels set in, a virtual zoo lived comfortably above us among outdated satin bedspreads, racks of long forgotten evening gowns, and lonesome toys. A well-used croquet set triggered memories of tulip teas and mouthwatering pink ladies. My dad's toboggan lay warped in a dark corner next to unused ski apparel that was purchased in the event we were invited to Skytop Lodge. Dusty tennis rackets anticipated impromptu matches that never occurred. How did our unconventional American Dream devolve into a tragic comedy that would have intrigued Tennessee Williams and Red Skelton?

## "I love Tea and Honey more than you."

My maternal grandparents played a considerable role in my family's life. Milton was fondly referred to as Pops and Theresa was lovingly called Momps. My grandfather drove to our house in his shiny black Cadillac on weekends and worked on the landscaping and masonry. He completed as much as he could and hired skilled laborers to finish the rest. Making our house the showcase of the neighborhood was his pet project. Momps often helped with cleaning, cooking, and caring for me, her cherished granddaughter. The five of us spent hours in each other's company throughout the seasons. We barbecued, swam, relaxed in the sun, romped in piles of leaves, cuddled by the fire, threw snowballs, played cards, celebrated holidays, and made up some of our own, or simply planned for the future. It seemed as if life was about as good as it could get. Milt was a partner in a printing business and enjoyed a comfortable lifestyle. Ultimately, Claude was forced to run his family's newspaper. Like many dreamers, my father's goal in life was to have a million bucks in the bank by the time he was thirty. He was pretty close to achieving his objective when destiny began creeping around every corner.

Milton and Grace Kennedy, my maternal grandparents, on their way to Bermuda.

I was about three years old when dad started falling down without a moment's notice. It might occur as my parents took a romantic stroll on the beach or he'd suddenly fly down the basement stairs. I can't conceive of how my mother felt when doctors informed her that a portion of her young husband's spine was disintegrating. Dad was in the hospital for more than a year after a team of surgeons chiseled bone chips from his hips and rebuilt his backbone into an inflexible rod. None of the medical personnel at the hospital knew my father was allergic to iodine. A few days after the operation they watched in horror as dad's skin collapsed around the foot long incision in his back. That is when our lives changed beyond our wildest nightmares.

Milt and Theresa lost their eldest daughter in a gruesome car accident when my mom was only six years old. They couldn't handle being around anyone who was suffering with a major illness, the possible loss of a family member, or God forbid, both. Pathetically, my mom, dad, and I were now classified as a group of undesirables. My universe crumbled as my precious grandparents withdrew themselves from our lives. My mother was devastated. She literally lived at the hospital and could no longer care for me. In a few weeks' time, I went from being the darling of the family to an orphan of sorts. Ma hired an elderly Swedish couple named Tea and Honey to look after me. From that moment on, I rarely saw my mother for more than a year. I didn't see Momps and Pops again for what seemed an eternity.

Tea was a tiny bespectacled lady who wore a never ending series of flowery blue dresses. Honey was a blonde giant of a man who wore a navy pin striped suit no matter what weather conditions prevailed. Their accents were so thick that it was a chore to understand them. I often relied on the expressions in their gentle eyes and gestures to figure out what they were saying. They were childless and showered their love upon me. Tea and Honey became much more than my nannies. My mother and I would have been lost without them.

Mom came home at dawn each day to bathe and change before returning to the hospital where she sat and cat napped by my unconscious father's side. My mother left Tea and Honey's weekly wages by the toaster each Sunday. They never took their salary until ma left the next week's money. They wanted to be sure she had enough to pay the bills.

I became a very lonely little girl in a virtually empty house. My new caregivers had the sense to acquire some child-sized furniture so I could at least sit comfortably. With their own money they bought a wooden musical rocking chair. Classical chimes consoled me as I moved back and forth with my solemn and confused thoughts. They also purchased a fabulously modern easy chair. It had a curved, black, wrought iron frame with a fuchsia canvas cover which supported me like a big hug. I spent endless hours watching television in that secure seat. Tea was actually proud of me when I became a human TV Guide. She'd utter a time of day or night and I'd recite what was on the tube.

Nothing improved when my father finally came home. Tea and Honey stayed on during the transition. Our dining room with its sculpted crimson carpet, snow-colored satin curtains, and shiny candelabras was converted into a rehabilitation center. No one was allowed to make a sound as dad recuperated in his seemingly enormous hospital bed.

One spring day as I played by myself in the grotto I decided to run around the house for the fun of it. As I turned the corner, I saw my father awake and semi-vertical for the first time since I lost him so many months ago. He was wearing a white cotton undershirt and boxer shorts. His legs were curled under him. Even at my tender age, I knew they were completely useless. Two burly male attendants supported him. Dad was barely able to lift his head but he made an effort to look at me. I assumed he was too weak to talk because all I remember was a shocking silence. Tea and Honey eventually faded out of the picture. My mother was a shadow and my father was a crippled ghost. Kindergarten was going to be a welcomed change.

# "I guess I'm not getting that tiara."

My mother surely loved my father. However, I'm positive that his family's fortune had a lot to do with her accepting his marriage proposal. Heck, Virginia Joan Bennett lived a few apartments down the block from my youthful mom. Rumor has it that Joan's mother was notorious for trying to marry off her daughter to a well-to-do individual. Joan married Ted Kennedy. My grandmother was no different. Theresa took one look at my tall, dark, handsome and stinking rich dad and saw visions of grandeur. It seemed that none of those ladies received the memo that marrying for prestige and opulence generally leads to a broken heart, embarrassing outbursts, and various addictions.

My dad hailed from an affluent family in Scarsdale, New York. Their mansion's estate included roomfuls of priceless art, formal and informal gardens, orchards, tennis courts, a kennel, acres of virgin forest, a generous pond, and a private illegal gas station. Sadly, Grandpa Herbert was a compulsive gambler who wagered his entire fortune on a horse race. He was up to his neck in scandals on a regular basis. Herb embezzled wealthy widows at the luxurious Westchester Country Club and hocked my grandmother's jewelry and sterling silver tea sets and flatware without ever considering her fragile sensibilities. Grandpa should have lived a life of luxury until the day he died. For decades he ran his father's highly profitable financial newspaper business and allegedly was part of the brains behind the creation of the original Standard and Poor's Index. Instead, he departed from this Earth penniless and alone in a rundown nursing home in Yonkers, New York.

Grandma Elizabeth a.k.a. Betsy was also made of money. She was a proud member of The Daughters of the American Revolution. According to my mother, this entitled me to the same honor and also afforded me the opportunity to attend gatherings at The New York Young Republican Club. She was thrilled at the prospect. I was deeply disturbed by such possibilities.

Elizabeth lost her mind by the age of forty. Relatives claimed it was early onset Alzheimer's disease. Rumors spread that she was driven mad by shame and gossip. I recently found a two inch thick black leather genealogical text which she paid to have researched and bound. It traced her ancestors back hundreds of years. Grandma's relatives ranged from prim ministers in New England to a gang of notorious horse thieves who were slaughtered during their one and only attempt to conquer England. Betsy ended up with a bandit any way you look at it.

Mom and dad told me that Elizabeth was an uncommunicative, stern, cold witch before her mind turned to gruel. It was her way or the highway. Both of her sons and only daughter rebelled against their mother's strictness. Grandma's offspring had everything money could buy except loving parents. Herbert was rarely home as he was too busy neglecting his wife, smoking pipes, swindling defenseless little old ladies, and playing the ponies.

Ma didn't fully realize that dad's parents were tragic individuals until a few years after their marriage. My mother may as well have obtained restraining orders against almost everyone in my father's family. I rarely interacted with them after she got to know them. The principals at my schools even had orders never to release me to any of "those people."

When Claudine walked up the aisle with Claude, she clearly expected to be taken care of like a princess for the rest of her days. The disappointment and incredulity of marrying into a clan of poverty-stricken lunatics was daunting. She gave up all hope of ever owning a diamond tiara. Mom ended up praying for a healthy husband whose legs would obey him.

# Chapter 3

## "More finger paint, please."

My father relearned how to walk during my first year at school. I discovered that I was absolutely thrilled to get the hell out of my house and associate with a devoted young woman, my teacher, and other normal people. Unfortunately, my mother's absenteeism as a guiding light in my life was now transformed into a smothering love Mother Theresa would have rejected. Dad was completely absorbed in his therapy at home. As a result, mom had some spare hours on her hands for the first time in a couple of years. I was the target now.

I remember joyful hours of busily slopping finger paint onto my vanilla colored rectangle of paper and cheerfully chatting with my kindergarten classmates. How liberating to be around individuals of my own age. And, there wasn't a freaking hospital bed in sight. Best of all, I could speak in an audible volume. There was one disconcerting drawback. Mother never left the front of the school during my entire morning session of newly found companionship. I'd peek out of the classroom window only to spot a gorgeous buxom blonde sitting alone in her sleek black Thunderbird. Ma's car was the only one on the street for the entire three hour period. When the dismissal bell rang, I dragged my newly rejuvenated body into the clutches of Claudine and was driven back to Doomsville, USA, my home. I counted the hours until I returned to my only source of delight, "Learning for Little Ones."

Dad was able to walk again by the time I entered first grade. However, he was not able to sit down for another year and wore a large, thick, gray back brace with steel stays which cut into his skin. For years he was laced into that hideous form of support like a modern day Victorian mannequin in drag. Father bore his painful burden without complaints. He gave a new and deeper meaning to the word stoic. I, on the other hand, grieved loudly over the fact that I had been handed over to a series of insane nuns during my sentence at Bronxville's St. Joseph's Elementary School.

Now that dad was literally on his feet again and miraculously back at work, good old Momps and Pops decided it was safe to re-enter our lives. My grandparents actually resided in Bronxville proper in a thoroughly enchanting apartment in the Midland Gardens complex. Their home was a mere five minute walk to St. Joe's. After too much deliberation, I was given permission to scurry home from school to Momps' flat. We even had sleepovers. This was a novel avenue of liberation for a reclusive second grader. Another factor in my favor was the enormous Polish school crossing guard who sidelined as a server at my grandparents' dinner parties. Hence, my safety was ensured as my mother was petrified I'd be splattered under a bus if left to my own devices.

My grandma and grandpa were back in my life. I was out of my house for more extended periods of time and my mother's social life was really taking off. Ma discovered the bliss of playing bridge with her pretty girl friends and swilling vodka until 6:15 p.m. when dad's train rolled into the station. My folks continued drinking as my Swanson's Turkey Dinner baked. I was left alone to pursue memorizing the <u>TV Guide</u>. Life continued to unfold in small dysfunctional increments.

# "Let's go to the circus and have your tonsils removed."

My parents always put their own unusual spin on special occasions and holidays. They customarily treated me to Ringling Bros. and Barnum & Bailey Circus for my birthday. That's when I fell in love with turtles. Along with the Cracker Jacks dad and I always shared, vendors sold individual baby turtles in a thin cardboard box with a cellophane window so you could observe your purchase before it died. After my birthday present succumbed, my mother dutifully accompanied me to Bronxville's one and only dingy pet store. We simply had to figure out what the hell it took to get an immature red-eared terrapin to live longer than a few weeks. Over a period of a couple of years and many deaths later, I became a veritable herpetologist and singlehandedly raised twelve healthy specimens of various species and sizes.

One sweltering day in July I decided that my reptilian pets deserved to stretch their limbs and experience an aquatic adventure. Our puny unheated pool seemed to be the perfect choice for their outing. When my mother came home from shopping, she did a double-take as she spotted my green beauties swimming in a state of rapture. I was told in no uncertain terms that my cold-blooded companions should frolic in a more suitable environment. The next deepest opportunity was my father's bathtub. It was overcrowded but I believe my turtles enjoyed themselves even if it was a one shot deal. Ma made me scrub that tub with Comet, a green powdery cleanser, until my hands looked like a manual laborer's.

Months later in the cold of winter and with turtles in mind, Claude and Claudine were positive that I would get dressed in a flash at any time of the day or night if they offered me an opportunity to attend the "Greatest Show on Earth." They also knew that I would have an actual smile on my face which was a genuine bonus. My parents could rest assured that I'd even allow my mother to button me up in her favorite choice of outerwear. On one occasion that is painfully etched in my memory, I wore a black velvet coat with white satin lining. Mom fastened my matching headgear with a bow under my chin. It fit like a barnstormer's leather flying cap and was decorated with ermine tails which hung by my ears. I'd suffer almost any humiliation for the chance to cheer for trapeze artists, eat cotton candy, and buy another hard-shelled companion.

With this knowledge in hand, my owners used the "must-see attraction for fans of all ages" as a ploy. The three of us sped off in dad's black Buick sedan with cherry red leather seats. I had memorized the general directions to New York City's Madison Square Garden. We were not headed that way. The next thing I knew I was being stripped in a hospital bed. I was a basket case because I was terrified that my parents had lied to me. No one explained what was going on as I was strapped down and rolled into an operating room. I recalled the initial effects of anesthesia in the mint green tile surgical center but nothing more until I awoke in my folks' bed. I felt woozy for days. It was as if there were tiny razor blades in my throat when I swallowed. My mother and father fed me spoonfuls of raspberry sherbet, my dad's favorite dessert. I grew to like it or I would have starved to death. As I healed I wondered what in God's name had happened. Many months later I discovered that my tonsils had been removed. Gee, I wonder why I didn't trust my parents' decisions as I matured.

When I did rely on their judgment it turned out to be wrong on quite a number of occasions. My parents still took me to the circus on my birthday for two more years but it had somehow lost its charm. We began travelling to Playland Amusement Park in Rye, New York. This captivating outdoor recreational area has been a favorite family stomping ground since 1928. The unnerving "Dragon Coaster" still serves as its mascot and is one of approximately one hundred wooden roller coasters still in operation in the United States. I was very disappointed that I was too short to ride this famous monster. Dad decided that an appropriate alternative would be to hop aboard "The Wild Mouse." We were the only people on line for this excursion into hell. That should have been a hint right there.

My father and I innocently lowered ourselves into a metal rodent. Much to our dismay we travelled faster than the speed of light on rickety tracks that were stacked sky high. I sat in the front of our solitary car between my father's legs. We careened around sharp curves which gave us the impression that we were going to die every few seconds. I panicked and ripped tiny handfuls of hair from my dad's lower limbs which were plastered around my petite frame. The pain was so excruciating that he wailed like a banshee. A crowd gathered below "The Wild Mouse" as Claude and Little Claudie hurtled through the air. People were attracted by blood curdling screams. My father turned out to be the biggest attraction at Playland that day.

# Chapter 4

## "He only wants half your net worth."

My father was mistakenly informed by his doctors that he would never be able to work again after his near fatal back operation. They weren't aware of his tenaciousness. Sadly, dad was in a state of acute pain for years. I witnessed one of the paralyzing seizures he succumbed to when I walked into my parents' bedroom one Saturday morning. From the waist down, my father shuddered in agony as if his legs were in an earthquake. Stunned, I asked if I could help in any way. Dad calmly stated that this was the way it was for him and gripped a pillow as if in childbirth. He explained that he frequently fell into the arms of unsuspecting but always compassionate fellow passengers during his commute to work. He would have collapsed if left unattended.

I thought of the trek my father took twice a day, Monday through Friday. My mother drove him to the train which left Bronxville at 8:00 a.m. After arriving at Grand Central Station in bustling New York City, he boarded a rumbling and bumpy subway to Rector Street and *walked* to his office. He then ran a business as best he could. I often asked myself, "How in God's name did he make it all those years?" Yet, he always got off that homebound train smiling because he had managed to become an admired and sought after friend of every beer guzzling/bridge playing young executive in the Club Car. He gave mom a peck on the cheek and we cruised home for dinner. Perhaps that was the most difficult part of his day.

My voguish mother's cooking made <u>I Love Lucy's</u> meals look like Julia Child's culinary creations. Ma prepared three types of chicken. "American Chicken" was just plain broiled chicken. You were lucky if you got a plastic salt shaker on the table. "Italian Chicken" consisted of a blob of tomato paste and a wad of mozzarella cheese on a piece of poultry which transformed into a solid burnt pyramid as the temperature in the broiler increased. "French Chicken" involved half of a canned peach on a leg or breast and a drizzling of sucrose laden syrup. Praise the Lord for Ronzoni side dishes of canned spaghetti and macaroni. Our frozen vegetable intake consisted of a pool of partially thawed string beans or peas swimming alongside the aforementioned carbohydrates. Along with these delectable meals, the stench of mom boiling our poodle's entrée of chicken livers with onions, peppercorns, and a bay leaf permeated the house. The pièce de résistance was my school lunch. It was packed in one of those un-sealable wax paper bags which encouraged air to harden my, drum roll please, bread and butter sandwich.

My father's mobility continued to progress due to weekly acupuncture treatments. Implausible as it seems, he recovered to the extent that he played golf with his cronies on Saturday mornings. Dad rarely made it out of the high nineties but everyone appreciated what an amazing comeback he'd made. My father golfed at the Westchester Country Club in Rye, New York. Every now and then he played with a celebrity or a politician such as the New York State Boxing Commissioner or an attorney general.

One afternoon dad arrived home with bags of unusable cosmetics after golfing with Dick Clark who was pushing his new line. On another occasion my father complained that he played with an "unruly actor who had the nerve to wear jeans on the golf course." The accepted attire was an Izod sports shirt and madras pants. The actor's arms were "covered with unsightly tattoos" which made dad cringe. I almost fainted when my father nonchalantly explained that he spent the whole day with Sean Connery! Sean was at the height of his fame. Goldfinger was the number one movie in the nation. James Bond was my personal favorite fantasy man. My friends and I salivated over his escapades. For heaven's sake, dad drove us to the local movie theater and listened to our blathering for countless weekends. In my juvenile opinion, not telling me Sean Connery was accessible was akin to a grisly crime.

My adolescent grumblings were the least of my father's problems. He had prostate and kidney surgery shortly after the Bond incident. Manhattan's eminent Memorial Sloan-Kettering Cancer Center called our home on Christmas Eve regarding dad's test results. I was the unlucky person who answered the phone. The nitwit on the line told me to please inform my father that he had cancer of the kidney and to be sure to have a happy holiday season. Ho, ho, ho! In January, astute surgeons informed us that dad's filtering organ was so diseased that it appeared to be malignant. It actually wasn't but it had to be removed in any case. That news brought great relief and became a belated Christmas gift. Too bad malpractice lawsuits weren't a fad yet. Dad would have made his elusive million bucks and then some.

A few years later, my father almost died again from "the nastiest hernia we've seen in ages because it leaked poison into his system. The worst was a monk's whose scrotum hung down to his knees. Mr. Seibert's was a close second." Such captivating news to hear from doctors as dad recovered in an intensive care unit for the thousandth time. The nurses loved mom and me. I had a steady supply of two Evian bottles filled with vodka in my handbag. Everyone thought we were the most upbeat relatives they'd ever encountered even though we were in the direst of circumstances.

Hospital stays didn't compare to what my maternal grandfather did to dad. Pops was an Irish dandy who often imbibed to an excess at home after losing his eldest daughter in a drunken driving accident. He was also a pompous, greedy, and devious man at times. When Pops was out with clients at a restaurant, he used to pay the bartender to serve him ginger ale when he ordered a scotch and soda. My granddad usually made a killing at these meetings because he was the only sober one at his table of unsuspecting business associates.

Pops co-owned a printing company. Well into his career, he conjured up a scheme to oust his partner and take over the enterprise. My grandfather's colleague discovered the malevolent plan and legally dismissed him from the firm. Pops was getting on in years and had nowhere to turn except to my family. Out of love for my mother, dad reluctantly brought him into his family's longstanding financial newspaper business. By this time, dad owned an entire ancient building on Rector Street in downtown New York City. He reigned over floor after creaky floor of administrative offices and presses and enjoyed an excellent relationship with the NYC Printers' Union. My father was often generous to a fault and also employed his older brother, Ted, and a few elderly aunts.

Pops took over running the printing sector. Within a short period, he decided to change the quality of paper the chronicle was printed on which made the cost of publication skyrocket. The Union men hated my arrogant grandpa and went on strike. They came back to work only after dad pleaded with them. Pops repented but stated that the only way he could really work productively was if he owned the entire division. Ma convinced my father to sell all of his printing presses to my self-serving granddad for the sum of one dollar.

The business took a nose dive. Dad was losing his shirt. The sole way to attempt to recover from this mess was to concede to Pops' coercion. My father was forced to buy back his own presses from my covetous grandfather for an enormous sum of money. My grandparents were set for life and dad was in a state of financial ruin. Momps and Pops decided to add insult to injury. Once again, my family was spiraling to the ground in a ball of fire. My mother's own flesh and blood reverted to their vile trick of dismissing us as unworthy. Our phone rang two years later when Pops was diagnosed with terminal cancer.

## "Stay back ten feet: I'm radioactive."

Claude, Claudine, Muffy II, and I arrived at my grandparents' apartment within moments of the announcement of Milton's poor prognosis. He was given less than a year to live; he hung on for five. Mom rarely left his side and comforted him to the very end. Each evening my saintly father took a cab from the train station to meet us at my grandparents so we could spend quality time together.

We returned to Sloan-Kettering for Pops' treatments. I know I'd never allow anyone to pack my lungs with glowing pellets. I often wondered what went through my grandfather's head when he read the laminated bracelet on his wrist with its brutal command printed in capital letters, "STAY BACK TEN FEET; I'M RADIOACTIVE." My mother became hysterical each time she walked into his hospital room and saw my grandmother sitting on a chair casually chain smoking between full oxygen tanks. It would have been easier on everyone if they had been blown to bits right then and there.

During the final year of my grandfather's life, my mother had my room redecorated by someone who must have been tripping on acid. My red, white, and pink childhood bedroom was transformed as if by witchcraft into something that resembled a blue and green plastic opium den. Silver dollar sized aqua and lime colored beads hung vertically to the floor from the inside of both doors making it impossible to enter or leave in a silent manner. A forest green glass cone dangled from the ceiling by intertwined gold chains. It provided just enough light to walk across the room. Reading was out of the question. My bookcase and desk were replaced with shimmering chartreuse pillows that were strewn uninvitingly upon the pea green wall-to-wall carpet. Mint colored sheer curtains billowed from the blast of my air conditioner which was on twenty-four hours a day. I hoped if it was cold enough my parents wouldn't grace me with their presence.

I was expecting to hear a friend's voice when my avocado Princess phone rang on Christmas Eve. It was my misfortune to inform my mother that her father had passed away. To this day, I have never observed anyone get dressed so quickly and efficiently. She slapped on flaming red lipstick, brushed her platinum blonde hair, sprayed on enough Chanel No. 5 to choke a moose, zipped up a chic long-sleeved black velvet dress with a plunging décolletage trimmed with black lace, stepped into a pair of black velvet stilettos, and wrapped long strands of pearls around her neck. She screamed for me to get my drab navy Loden coat. We sped through icy streets in her pale yellow Cutlass convertible.

When we arrived at my grandparents' home, ma couldn't believe her dad was gone. My mother knelt and spilled her beaded black velvet clutch onto the carpet in order to get her compact. I thought it was rather inappropriate to powder her nose at such a dreadful moment. However, mom placed her compact's mirror under Pops' nose to see if he was still breathing. I guessed she'd seen that method of determining death on a soap opera. Ma continued screaming, "He's alive! He's alive!" until I convinced her that her fingerprints were making smudges which appeared to be his distant life force. It was a tedious night and a miserable holiday season.

A highlight of my grandfather's funeral was the opportunity to meet one of my mother's former beaux. Joe was a handsome, well-dressed, rather short Italian man who became a filthy rich land developer in Florida. He cheated left and right on his poor wife who had blessed him with two sons. I knew instinctively he'd take my mother away from us in a flash, even during the service, if she gave him any encouragement. I felt sorry for my pauper of a father.

We were packed liked sardines in a limousine which Joe insisted on paying for as we drove to Gate of Heaven Cemetery in Hawthorne, New York. Dad knew he had nothing to worry about because mom's middle name was "loyal." Once ma devoted herself to you, you couldn't shake her loose no matter what you did. However, my mother's pet peeve was lying. She advised me, "I can understand murdering someone because you might have had a bad day, but I can't tolerate a liar. Once you've lost trust in someone, that's it." My dad never lied to her.

My mother and grandmother exchanged Kleenex boxes during the holiday season after Milt's demise. Consequently, ma insisted on throwing a sizable soiree on ensuing Christmas Eves to keep Momps from thinking about Pops. At this point, even the cops were getting tired of us.

# Chapter 5

## "You'll be a social failure if you don't learn how to play bridge."

It appeared that we were related to the Prince and Princess of Monaco in spite of the fact that my parents didn't have two nickels to rub together. In the fall and winter months, mom dazzled her admirers with a tourmaline stole and a white mink coat. I'll never forget when ma's beloved albino treasure was stolen during one of several grand thefts at our home in Bronxville/Yonkers. You would have thought that her best friend had moved to the Moon. Dad must have hocked some remaining articles from his folks' apartment in order to purchase another fabulous fur for his sorrowful spouse. Mom's face fell to the ground as she dragged a full-length ranch mink coat from a gigantic box. She was disappointed that it wasn't the color of freshly fallen snow. Sometimes I just wanted to shake some sense into her especially when I saw the look on my father's face. He even had it monogrammed with her initials in gold thread. Each time mom begrudgingly donned her mammalian pelts, she remarked how dark and lack luster dad's offering was. It was the last mink coat she ever owned.

Mother continued to attend her afternoon card parties. In between bidding and tricks, she tried to convince me that I would be a social failure if I didn't play bridge, tennis, and golf. I willingly took tennis lessons and quickly earned the required red, white, and blue ribbons for learning the basic forehand and backhand strokes, and how to serve. Ma didn't stand a chance at teaching me how to play bridge. I had no interest at the time. I dutifully attended golf sessions but was asked to withdraw from my first tournament because I lost so many balls. I could swim and dive like a fish but evidently my aquatic talents were of no social merit.

To my utter despair, my mother demanded that I partake in not one but three debutante cotillions. I was instructed that my escorts would be provided and none of my friends would be allowed to attend. An expensive gown was chosen for me at Bergdorf Goodman's which is a luxurious department store on Fifth Avenue in New York City. Ma's hairdresser was scheduled to perfect my coiffure at the house before the event. Even though I was an ungrateful teenager, it was apparent to me that my mother was attempting to vicariously experience the debut she had been denied. Mom was bitterly disappointed by my lack of enthusiasm. That didn't stop her from designing a petal pink, silk, strapless, form fitting evening gown with a modest fish tail. The cherry on the cake of her striking costume was a six foot long matching stole with a six inch wide ostrich feather cuff on one end of the wrap. She looked stunning. I looked depressed.

The neighbors across the street had a long lost cousin who was a dentist from Pennsylvania. My parents decided that he would be a suitable escort for me even though they had never laid eyes on him. He could have been Jack the Ripper's descendant for all they knew. This gregarious guy showed up in the required tuxedo and a hideous Beatle wig down to his shoulders. My folks almost had a stroke until he removed the mop top and suggested that we all take a gander at his new black Porsche 911. Since he appeared to be relatively well-heeled, all was forgiven over a few cocktails.

Dad arranged to have his newspaper's photographer at my coming out party at the Westchester Country Club. Hundreds of shots were taken of all of my parents' friends. They had a blast. I felt as if my initiation was a grueling, wasteful, and torturous charade.

Unbeknownst to me, another unveiling was in the works. A few weeks later, I was presented to a mighty cardinal at the Apawamis Club in Rye, New York. To my disgust, I learned that a cardinal is a Roman Catholic dignitary who is next in rank to the pope. My pre-arranged date was a strapping young football player who just happened to be the son of one of mom's bridge buddies. We met for the first time at the gala.

The hairdresser was called to our home once again in order to prepare for the second atrocity. The limousine was ready to go and I was fit to be tied. A few minutes before we departed, I excused myself and walked into the Bar Room of our house where every liquor known to humanity was stored. I opened a bottle of tequila and chugged a fourth of it. I calmly tightened the cap and slid into the rented vehicle next to my grandmother. Within a short time, I began dissolving into Momps' side. My head rested upon her shoulder. My brain felt as if it was trapped inside a tornado. By the time we got to our destination, I could barely walk.

My parents couldn't figure out what the hell was wrong with me. Evidently, I was introduced to my handsome quarterback. Dad's photographer situated our party in front of a flagpole with a grand golf course at our backs. Just as he began clicking away, I passed out as if I was filming a segment of <u>Rowan & Martin's Laugh-In</u>. Mom was furious that I was ruining her night. After a dozen cups of coffee and dinner, I was presented to one of the pope's right hand men. There is photographic evidence of me with bedraggled hair, bloody scrapes on my arm, and silk flowers missing from the bodice of my dress. I steadfastly refused to kiss the cardinal's ring and put a lip lock on my own hand. I still get a kick out of those shots. I had been tortured for years by nuns and priests. I certainly wasn't going to change my tune because of a sham known as my entrance into society.

Good God Almighty! Two weeks later, I was scheduled to appear at a televised international debutante ball. How in the world were my parents paying for all of this crap? We ate freaking fish sticks for dinner but somehow could afford gowns galore, luxurious limousines, and parties for hundreds of people. Our life didn't make sense. Priorities, intuition, and common logic were consistently replaced with materialism, illusion, fallacies, and gallons of booze; not to mention maxed out credit cards and oodles of loans.

For once my pleading actually worked. I got out of that potential public disaster by the skin of my tequila stained teeth. Claude and Claudine cancelled my proposed third cotillion. It was one of the wisest decisions they ever made.

## "You could have been a human potato chip!"

I loved my parents and grandparents very much. Yet, at a young age I was perplexed by their personal choices and social mores. Sure, I enjoyed swimming in the largest pool in Westchester County since I was most content when submerged. Of course, it was a pleasure to entertain at the villa on the hill. However, I didn't truly enjoy my parents' company until I was in my early twenties. At that point, I made two important compromises. In order to have Claude and Claudine in my life, I would no longer discuss politics, racism, sex, religion, alcoholism, drugs, or any topics more controversial than the weather, fashion, or equestrian events. Secondly, mom and dad would have no knowledge of my personal life. After all, ignorance is bliss. I came to these decisions after years of being forced to create falsehoods about whom I was really with and where I truly was. Unfortunately, in order to develop a social life as a teen, 99.9% of my comrades and I had to lie to our folks. The only other alternative was to acquire friends who were master liars and let them engineer deceitful acts.

I made the disconcerting observation that I had to look long and hard for a person of any color other than alabaster when I was with my parents. It was also next to impossible to associate with anyone who wasn't a Republican Catholic. I often asked myself, "Where are the Democratic Jews?" I led a sheltered life in my parents' grip until a magical neighborhood friend showed me that there was more to life than the prison walls of my little world. Sadly, my narrow minded father nicknamed her Svengali.

Partying became my newly discovered passion. Look at my role models. How could I be blamed for inheriting "fun genes" in my DNA? Mom and dad were often at festivities until all hours of the night. For God's sake, they were gone for three days come New Year's Eve. They reserved a room at The Westchester's Main Club and returned home much paler but in good spirits.

A few times a year my parents travelled to conventions for dad's business. The opportunities for merrymaking in their absence were bountiful especially since my lenient chaperone was Meg. This dear woman was my father's sixty-two inch, elderly, obese, red headed receptionist. About thirty minutes before droves of my wild friends arrived at my parentless abode, I fastidiously prepared a feast in the master bedroom where Meg stayed. Plates of every cookie and treat imaginable and a bucket of ice containing a liter of ginger ale and a quart of vanilla ice cream were placed within easy reach of her plump fingers. I turned on the television, deposited Muffy on her bed, and locked them in for the night. I shudder when I recall my actions. I could have been brought up on negligent homicide charges if Meg needed medical attention. In fact, it's a bloody miracle she lived through my last bash.

Upstairs was off limits except for those couples who slyly slipped passed me. A handsome Greek friend became amorous with his date while smoking a cigarette on my bed. Apparently, they unknowingly left behind a smoldering Marlboro in the middle of my mattress. Thank God I went upstairs to freshen up because that is when I smelled something acrid. I opened the door to my boudoir and found a wall of smoke. My first thought was that I was responsible for the probable deaths of Meg and Muffy. I couldn't even see the lock on their door. I opened windows, turned on the air conditioner, and raced back and forth from my father's bathroom with a tumbler of water about fifty times before the smoke subsided. I crept into Meg's room and breathed a sigh of relief because she and my pup were still alive. The French doors which led to a terrace were wide open. I nudged both of them just to be sure that they weren't in smoke induced comas.

Needless to say, I slept in the guest room that night. The next morning I explained to Meg what had happened because the house smelled like Smokey the Bear's suburban nightmare. We dragged my mattress onto the patio, cut out the burned part, and let it breathe in the fresh air for five days before we replaced it in my room. We were amateurs. I now know that I should have purchased a new one.

When my parents returned from their trip, Meg and I welcomed them with open arms. The moment mom walked into the house, she sniffed the air and marched directly up to my room like there was a homing device planted there. She flipped the mattress and began screaming, "What the hell happened here? You could have been a human potato chip!" Ma actually hugged me after I tearfully recounted the ridiculous truth about a forbidden coupling in my chamber. She was thankful that we were all alive and the house hadn't burned to the ground. Meg never took care of me again.

# "Don't worry; there won't be that many people at Woodstock."

Meg was gone but my lying didn't cease. A Fordham University mixer was my code name for a rendezvous at a jazz club in Manhattan. A movie and hamburger in my hometown were actually a few drinks at a bar called Pops on Gunhill Road in the Bronx where affable numbers runners congregated. A sleepover with my high school girlfriends was a dance-a-thon at a Brazilian hot spot in Greenwich Village.

My friends and I never ventured out for an evening of entertainment before 9 p.m. As I got older, we didn't bother to arrive in New York City before 11 p.m. Therefore, it was impossible to conclude a fun-filled outing of laughter, dancing, eating, and drinking before twilight. Eventually, I gave up trying to sneak into my room at 5 a.m. with those damn plastic beads banging on my bedroom door and my parents stopped trying to enforce a curfew. Years of screaming, crying, and fighting among Claude, Claudine, and Little Claudie prevailed before that goal was finally achieved. The problem was that Little Claudie wasn't so little any more.

I desperately wanted to attend the now famous Woodstock Festival. Many of my pals planned to travel to Max Yasgur's dairy farm but I was forbidden to do so. My parents were dead set against my going as they imagined me violated in front of a band of psychotic rock stars that were tripping on acid. A group of masterful deceivers put their heads together to devise a strategy for me to be present at this historical event.

My dad received a phone call from a young man I barely knew a few days before everyone's departure. I would venture to say that Ricky is most likely residing at Sing Sing Correctional Facility because of his fraudulent tendencies. This trickster posed as his own father and spun a tale that I even believed. The supposed patriarch of Ricky's family bantered with my father about the stock market, what it was like to raise kids, and the cost of country estates in upstate New York. They were chums by the time they got off the phone. I learned that Ricky's uncle owned a summer retreat not far from the musical celebration and that I would be staying at his spacious home. There was even a lake on the property; nice touch. I was astounded by Ricky's expertise and that a network of lifelong liars had come to my rescue.

I was elated as I waved goodbye to my parents and drove off in an enormous beat up blue Chevy with four of my girlfriends. We proceeded to sit in the mother of all traffic jams in stifling heat. I wanted to go home before we got there. After hours on the road, we arrived at the uncle's home where we met the pathological liar and about a dozen other chums. Ricky had actually included particles of truth in his tale. The problem with the manor was that no one had lived there for about twenty years. There were no windows because they had been shattered by vandals. Chards of glass lay upon the warped wooden floors. None of the doors locked. The lake in the backyard gave a new and deeper meaning to the word stagnant. Parts of the roof were missing and a zoo of small animals had clearly made this dump their home.

Everyone pitched in and set up sleeping bags, food and water centers, and candles all over the main room. There were no bathrooms or tubs to be found. I just wanted to hop in a cool shower and take a nap. Instead, we all headed for the campgrounds to see and hear our idols perform. I looked out of place in my Pucci print Empire dress with a mandarin collar and a seductive teardrop opening, high-heeled sandals, full make-up, and long bleached blonde hair. Ricky's house of horrors was about five miles from the center of action. We discovered that fact when our feet were practically bleeding.

I refused to walk another inch. Without thinking twice, I glommed onto the back of a slow moving cream colored Volkswagen Beetle. I dug my fingernails into the metal rim around the rear windshield and hung on for dear life. Both feet were wrenched sideways like an impaired dancer. My stilettos were precariously balanced on the fender of the VW Bug. I was virtually crippled by the time my ride ended.

All of my buddies had adopted similar hitchhiking postures. We convened by the side of the road, stretched our numbed legs, and headed into the heart of the activity along with 500,000 other young people. For openers, a curly haired bare-chested man grabbed me around the waist and planted a deep kiss upon my lips. I was stupefied. Fortunately, one of my protective male friends extracted me from the clutches of Don Juan. We proceeded to deposit ourselves deep within the territory of peace, love, and extremely loud music. For hours we soaked up every note our heroes played. My pals and I were sickened when we realized that we were listening to the humongous pulsating speakers of a rainbow colored van instead of the living legends we had come to hear. At the end of the day, we trudged home to collapse at our abandoned eyesore.

The gals whispered and giggled all night because it was too grotesque a place to safely lose consciousness. The guys snored and periodically questioned us as to how in God's name were we still talking to one another after so many arduous hours. The ladies of the house arose early due to a desperate desire to cleanse our filthy bodies. We actually bathed in that sewer of a pond. Good Lord that was the last straw. Three of us headed home that afternoon. There wasn't a soul on the road. Everyone in the universe was in Woodstock, stoned out of their minds in mudslides, and with an ear to a radio.

I was never so glad to see hot and cold running water in my life. My folks were ecstatic and astonished that their seemingly adventurous daughter had returned home from the biggest event in rock and roll history in less than forty-eight hours. Mom looked luminous and dad was having the time of his life. I had arrived at the perfect moment. It was the night of my parents' annual fete. Hundreds of people were in attendance. After lingering in a warm bath, I helped myself to a large plate of delicious food and a tasty drink from one of the bartenders. I headed for the terrace off my folks' bedroom on the second floor of the villa. I gazed bemusedly at the elegant beauties and handsome escorts with their cocktails and compared them to the city of throbbing blue jeans, naked breasts, and marijuana I had recently visited. There had to be a middle ground where I could comfortably reside.

I was fortunate to absorb the essence of two priceless events that summer. One would be recorded in history books. The other would be emblazoned in my mind as a unique memory of a lifestyle that was as strong as butterfly wings. Neither grand performance would occur again. Claude and Claudine's final soiree took place on the same weekend in August that the town of Bethel, New York became the transitory center of hippie counterculture.

My mother shimmying the night away.

## "I love you but I don't like you."

Sometimes I wondered if my parents regretted having me. I bet all kids, at one time or another, fall victim to that wretched thought during their childhood and adolescence. Nonetheless, some of my mother's snippets about her past didn't help the matter. Mom explained how she fainted one night while she danced at a party. Ma passed out because she was trying to hide her pregnancy in a sexy black dress. The snugness of her attire became intolerable for both of us. Mother stopped dancing for seven months after that experience and began wearing maternity clothes the next day. Now, why did I have to listen to that precious anecdote?

Sadly, mom suffered numerous miscarriages before she gave birth to me. I was "the last try." At the time, doctors were led to believe that Thalidomide, the fetus crippling drug, helped prevent premature births. Due to a miracle, ma ceased ingesting all medications and alcohol when she found out she was pregnant. Thank God she never smoked because I would have been born sans lungs. To this day I am amazed that I was brought into the world without an epidural, any pain killers, or liters of vodka.

When I entered this plane with all of my limbs intact, it was assumed that I possessed the almighty dance gene. Mom adored dressing me in pale pink tutus. Unfortunately, ballet lessons were not my cup of tea. Ma drove me to a rundown mansion in Bronxville which was owned by a former Russian ballerina. I still don't believe that she was anything more than an escaped convict from some Eastern European country. She was immensely overweight and had dark frizzy dyed hair. The windows of her home were painted black on the inside. When my mother and I rang the doorbell of this supposed dancer's sanctum, we heard a pack of hysterical dogs barking and the smell of urine assaulted our nostrils. Why the hell I was dragged there against my will for more than six months I'll never know.

A few years passed and ballroom dancing became the next hobby that was forced upon me. I yearned to associate with the young Protestants who attended

Bronxville Public School. I was envious that they attended coeducational classes and didn't wear uniforms every damn day of the school year. However, Barclay's and Miss Covington's Schools of Dance were far from the manner in which I envisioned myself intermingling with these attractive Waspy Democrats-in-training.

The only opportunity I had to mix with the legendary Titans was at The Bronxville Women's Club on Monday and Thursday evenings. Mom selected party dresses which I would have rather burned. I also had to wear anklets for the first season even though my fashionable peers wore nylons. Hiding between a wall and the refrigerator at my grandmother's abode was the only way I managed to miss a few of these humiliating sessions. In spite of it all, I am pleased to say that I am able to spring into a graceful waltz, lindy, box step, fox trot, or cha-cha-cha at any given moment.

As an adult I came to understand that ma's warped vision of my future reflected her own desires. She only wanted the best for me. Regrettably, her version of what was top notch was my ultimate nightmare. My mother's version of basic school transportation proves my point. It was a longstanding joke that a few of my friends and I arrived at The Ursuline Academy each morning in a decrepit black limousine. Our chauffeur's name was Johnny Dee. He was about seventy and had no business driving a vehicle because he was intoxicated 24/7. This booze hound's eyes gave a new and deeper meaning to the word bloodshot. He had so many bags under his peepers that plastic surgeons must have chased him with scalpels. Johnny smoked unfiltered Pall Malls until we choked and begged him to raise the glass window between us. After a semester, we didn't care anymore because we smoked more than he did.

Belittling my mother in public was a grave mistake which I tried to avoid at all costs. Unluckily, an incident involving my smoking in Johnny's vehicle was brought to my principal's attention. That nasty nun suspended me for a week. It was a perfect punishment. Staying at home with mom when she was peeved was akin to being locked in a cage with a malnourished jaguar.

When ma was upset about something, her anger didn't contain itself to the hours of daylight. After a few drinkies, her tongue cut like a knife. Mom rarely cursed in dad's presence. Both my father and I wished she had. Somehow, her verbal assaults would have been easier to take. Our brains were bleeding by the time my mother fell into a coma. During those hapless nights dad and I were unable to sleep because our hearts and minds were seared with pain. Ma always awakened the next morning with a convenient case of amnesia. She'd slide a comb through her platinum hair, slap on some ruby red lipstick, and zip into her full length black velvet and flesh colored lace dressing gown. Voilà, she resembled an untroubled queen. My father and I looked like we'd been beaten about the head with blunt instruments.

It turned out that dad was no angel either. He occasionally got mom to do his dirty work. When I was in seventh grade, my father declared that my waist length hair had to be hacked off to just above my shoulders. He was not fond of my Veronica Lake look-alike coiffure. My mother carried out his orders. I was grief-stricken and expressed that she had taken away "the only beautiful thing that was really mine." I guess she meant to console me but her response became a painful deposit in my memory bank. She stared at me and pronounced, "I love you but I don't like you." Morose became my middle name. That evening, Claudine just about murdered Claude.

The saying, "Everything that goes around comes around," is true. Whatever my mother dished out she received in spades from her mother. I'm positive that ma's parents' strained relationship adversely molded her tainted interpretation of familial love. My maternal grandmother lived in a stunning apartment. Yet, she was treated like a servant by her husband after their eldest daughter was basically murdered by a drunken driver. I believe my mom was hit the hardest when tragedy struck her family. Not only did she lose her only sister on that catastrophic night, but my grandparents never treated my mother with the love and respect she deserved after their precious teen was taken from them. It seemed that the Kennedys replaced young Grace with a deep sense of loss, a lack of compassion, deceit, and materialism.

My mother and grandmother adored me but they expressed their affection in very different ways. If there had been a contest for my adoration when I was growing up, Momps would have won hands down. She was an affectionate older woman who willingly played with me, created irresistible home cooked meals, and was at my beck and call. My grandma taught me how to be organized, responsible, didn't care how I looked, and revered me as a unique individual. The truth is that I have both of these memorable women to thank. The combination of my grandmother's redirected nurturing nature and my mother's love, ultimate loyalty, and passionate behavior made me who I am today.

The author's favorite photograph of ma et moi.

# Chapter 6

## "I kissed him and turned yellow."

My relationship with Claude and Claudine during most of my childhood and all of my teens could only be categorized as antagonistic. Our differences didn't solely revolve around my being an annoying person. It was as if we were from opposite ends of the solar system. I was a freaking gem compared to the offspring of many of my parents' friends. Yes, I lied in order to promote my social life but I didn't commit suicide or run away from home and I wasn't addicted to pills or heroin. A bond that had once tied us together was irrevocably altered after my dad's back operation. My grandparents' unceremonious rejections of us didn't help matters.

I remember having a short and prophetic conversation with my father when I was a youngster. We were in the living room in our home on a winter afternoon. Dad asked if I wanted to go to The Museum of Natural History in New York City. His invitation caught me off guard since I had accompanied him on rare occasions to the gas station, delicatessen, and newspaper stand. I was a mere child and my response was spontaneous and outrageous. I coolly replied, "I'd rather die." My father was rightfully stunned. A black cloud darkened his aura. He responded that he would never take me anywhere again and he rarely did, at least not to the places I wanted to go.

Shortly after Woodstock, I requested to be shipped off to a college on the west coast of the United States. California seemed to be a safe distance from my parents' scope of influence. My mom and dad had other plans. Without warning on a frosty Saturday in December, I was commanded to wear a dark gray wool suit with a gray fox collar, a form fitting black sleeveless turtleneck sweater, and black suede high heeled boots. My folks drove me to Chestnut Hill, Massachusetts. I was interviewed by some administrative hotshots at Pine Manor Junior College. It was a done deal as far as I could ascertain. I'd bet my front teeth that my grandmother had already sent a generous donation to the college in an effort to guarantee my entrance into this socially acceptable stomping ground for darling debutantes. I didn't look forward to continuing my higher education in the fall but at least I had one more summer in Bronxville before I officially left my parents' decaying nest.

As expected, a respectable amount of time elapsed before my mother and father gleefully handed me a shredded envelope with my letter of acceptance to Pine Manor. A rollicking summer ensued. I met a new fellow in town who was a prodigal son returning from California. I remember kissing him under a piano at a party one evening. No erotic pleasure was involved; we simply became semi-friends. Larry would sometimes walk me home from a neighborhood watering hole. He had the most unpleasant habit of vomiting about five minutes before we reached my door. I held his hand as he apologized and proceeded to empty the contents of his stomach. Larry often expressed his concern and confusion as to why he felt ill even though he had not ingested anything suspicious. As I readied myself for my new life in Massachusetts, I never gave puking Larry another thought.

I received a lengthy questionnaire relating to the compatibility of roommates from Pine Mattress, a well-deserved nickname. I drew a large "X" in red pen on every page and signed my name. To my surprise, I was assigned to a divine suite for two with a glorious private bathroom which consisted of a trio of adjoining rooms. My bright and sunny bedroom with a wall of closets was far away from my peers. It was located in an area with a private balcony, a large refrigerator, and tables which seated twelve. No one ventured to my heavenly wing of the building except to retrieve an occasional midnight snack.

My dearest friend since kindergarten attended Boston College which was about five minutes away by car. Her room was comparable to a cell at a local jail. Many of her new classmates were more like inmates. Pat moved into my dormitory in Chestnut Hill. Each week we observed trucks making deliveries to the refectory. They were packed with freshly baked goods, meats, fish, crisp vegetables, and loads of delectable fruits. Pat and I feasted like queens. We became especially fond of the chef's Eggs Benedict on Sundays. I opened a charge account at the school store and purchased music, colorful tights, and any supply that CVS or Walgreen's might carry. I chose English Literature as my major and Art History as my minor. I attended drawing and sculpting classes and read to my heart's content. I hated to admit it but life in Bean Town was most enjoyable and allowed me a sense of liberty which I had never known.

One evening as I applied mascara before a Stevie Wonder concert, I noticed that the conjunctiva, the white part of my eye, was yellow. I proceeded with my plans but felt nauseous throughout the night. I didn't cancel my weekend adventure to Amherst but almost passed out from the smell of gas when the bus needed to refill its tank. My usual energy level and willingness to participate in revelry reached an all-time low. I visited the infirmary when I returned to Chestnut Hill. A handsome Austrian doctor immediately quarantined me and contacted Claude and Claudine. They sped to my assistance, tucked me in the backseat of their Caddy, and brought me back home for three months of mandatory bed rest.

I couldn't believe how sick I felt. I lived in darkness, secluded in my bedroom, as I was unable to retain any solids in my system. I eventually discovered that small sips of milk with an occasional miniature Entenmann's chocolate chip cookie was the only meal that agreed with me. After about six weeks, concerned friends were allowed to visit but they had to remain outside in the cold. I conversed with them for a short while from my window on the second floor. I didn't have much strength to spare even for a quick laugh. My temperature did spike during one conversation when a buddy mentioned that dear mustard colored Larry had been diagnosed with hepatitis. However, he never took it easy and continued to drink. He supposedly looked like a cast member of <u>Night of the Living Dead</u>. Now I knew where I had picked up this debilitating ailment.

My blood was checked so often that the veins in my arms were no longer accessible to the nurses so they began poking the ones in my hands. By the time I was able to leave the house, I looked like a full-fledged junkie. The first opportunity I had to venture out after my prolonged illness was to my grandmother's. I relished each bite of her homemade mashed potatoes, pink applesauce, string beans, roasted pork tenderloin, sauerkraut, and my favorite dessert, rice pudding. Before my visit to Momps' dining room table, my doctor informed me that I was not allowed to drink any liquor or swallow any cough syrup with alcohol in it for one year. He made it perfectly clear that I would become extremely sick again if I allowed these forbidden liquids to touch my lips. The moron neglected to tell me that pork is one of the most difficult meats for the liver to synthesize. I became severely ill later that night and had to remain in bed for another week after grandma's delicious meal. My trust in the medical profession continued to dwindle at an alarming rate.

I saw Larry at a funeral about twenty years later. He had the gonads to ask me on a date. I hastily declined and inquired if he was going to give me consumption or cancer this time. He seemed bemused as usual.

I finally returned to Pine Manor and worked my ass off to graduate with my peers. That meant I had to take the maximum amount of credits allowed during the regular school year and attend both sessions of summer school. I was pleasantly surprised how sympathetic my professors were. My family was genuinely proud of me when I received my Associate of Arts degree as scheduled. I had to confess to my parents that Pine Manor had been an excellent choice for me because two years of intense studying was about as much as I could handle. Many of my friends had dropped out of college to travel or to marry but mostly because they couldn't tolerate it. I, on the other hand, had a legitimate sheepskin. I also had no intention of returning to New York.

## "Bean Town or bust!"

As chance would have it, I read an advertisement for typing and shorthand classes at Cambridge's Harvard University. I believed my folks would surely approve of my wish to better myself. Therefore, they would also grant permission for me to live with Pat who had rented an apartment with two other women on Commonwealth Avenue. Mom and dad agreed and my grandmother forked over the bucks to continue my education.

My morning and afternoon sessions at Harvard Summer School were conducted by a married couple who were professional musicians in a symphonic orchestra. The husband played the piano and helped develop the spherical ball of letters used in electric typewriters. I've never seen anyone type as fast as that man. His lovely wife was a cellist who taught me shorthand. I soaked up their lessons like a sponge and enjoyed every minute in their presence. I received valuable training that season and continue to use my knowledge of typing and shorthand every day.

Now that I possessed employable skills, my efforts to remain in Boston tripled. I found an attractive second floor studio apartment with an alcove, front hall, and two large closets. I returned to New York long enough to load up a small moving van with unessential furniture and utensils from the villa and headed back to Kelton Street in Allston, Massachusetts. I fondly remember sipping bourbon as I lovingly painted the intricate woodwork on the kitchen cabinets using an eye shadow brush while all of my belongings rested in a heap in the middle of the living room. My Dresden Blue and white kitchen was a masterpiece. Momps paid for the installation of cushiony, pale, silver gray wall-to-wall carpeting throughout my flat including the kitchen. I was never much of a cook. I hung rose colored satin drapes in the alcove window and covered my queen size bed with a matching spread. All of my lamps and furniture were gently used estate pieces. An enormous mauve silk sofa with six carved wooden legs culminating in lion's paws served as seating for my guests. I named my first apartment "The Puppy Palace." There wasn't a dog in sight.

I met my first boyfriend. He was a handsome Columbian graphic artist who was well respected around town. Art gallery openings, museum exhibits, concerts, parties, and trips to Cape Cod were side benefits. The highlight of our alliance was meeting his older sister who is one of my dearest friends to this day. Boston and Cambridge were safe places to mature because I was a young adult with no comprehension of mortality. If I had pulled the same crap in Manhattan, I would have been murdered in less than a week.

As my social life flourished, my father hired me to drum up subscriptions and advertisements for his newspaper. I made a solitary attempt to sell a trial run of his financial publication, was told to go to hell, and never picked up the phone again. I visited one agency with a handmade scrapbook of his clients. That endeavor also ended in failure. Dad was kind enough to issue me a salary for a considerable length of time and then thankfully yanked the plug on my fleeting and forgettable attempt to follow in his footsteps.

I began to search for a real job. After one interview, I was hired as an executive secretary at a small company which sold boiler burner units. They referred to themselves as heating specialists. There were two other women in the front office and a crew of truck drivers who were my fellow employees. I had very little to do but was well paid. The president and vice president of the firm were out on the road for most of the day so I took to reading literary classics to my work mates. When our employers returned from a site, they sometimes found their female staff weeping from a dramatic moment in a chapter that I had recited. Our bosses were ready to call in a team of psychiatrists during my theatrical rendition of <u>Camille</u> by Alexandre Dumas, fils.

I knew that being a secretary was merely a stepping stone but to what? I seriously considered becoming a professional basket weaver until I received a phone call from Svengali. She suggested that as a youngster I would have been nurtured in a Montessori environment instead of being manhandled by the clergy at my former schools. This wise and intuitive woman suggested that I investigate the possibility of becoming a Montessori teacher. Something clicked within my soul after researching the philosophy. This intuitive and loving lady who had brought me out of my stifling cave in Yonkers had now led me to an honored profession with a creative twist.

## "I succumbed to familial blackmail."

I had to acquire a Bachelor of Arts degree in any subject area except education in order to begin my Montessori indoctrination. The trainers didn't want to spend needless time deprogramming me. They just wanted a candidate with a well-rounded academic background. I succumbed to familial blackmail in order to attain my goal. Momps stated that she would pay for the rest of my schooling if I agreed to live with my folks and attend Manhattanville College in Purchase, New York.

Living with Claude and Claudine was bad enough but I had to grit my teeth as I enrolled in another Catholic school. At least most of the nuns didn't dress in habits anymore. I once again took the maximum amount of courses and attended both summer sessions. I continued to sculpt in metal, stone, and wax to maintain my sanity and even had an offer from an art gallery to display my pieces. I didn't have enough time to pump out a sufficient number of creations to make a name for myself but thanked them for their flattering invitation.

In order to preserve my brain cells, I often stayed at Pat's apartment in Manhattan. She had moved back to New York at about the same time I did in order to pursue a successful career in small leather goods. She frequently travelled to Italy and kindly offered me her flat to periodically escape my life of suburban drudgery. I also stayed with her during short breaks from school when she was back in town.

We still laugh as we recall our New York experiences in her building on the supposedly respectable Upper East Side. One evening as we sat in her living room by the opened windows leading to a fire escape, a man propelled himself onto her Oriental rug, stood up, hastily unlocked her front door, and ran down the hallway. We still had our drinks in our hands when a police officer jumped between us, tipped his cap, and ran after the perpetrator. Several months later, I answered her doorbell and was greeted by a lunatic holding a raised Bowie knife in an aggressive stance. I looked into his glazed eyes and informed him that we weren't serving hors d'oeuvres that evening so we wouldn't need any cutting utensils. I thanked him for his thoughtfulness, slowly removed the dagger from his hand, and threw it behind me. He then collapsed in an unconscious heap and pinned me to the floor. I screamed for Pat to get the odoriferous maniac off of me. We rolled him into the hallway, double locked the door, and hastily poured two glasses of Merlot.

Thanks to an iron will and Pat's support I graduated with my Bachelor of Arts degree in a year and a half and promptly moved to Washington, D.C. to begin my Montessori studies. I lived in a large townhouse on P Street and could walk to school in about twenty minutes. The other tenants were law students who pitied me because of the long hours I spent typing my teaching journals and creating time lines regarding evolution and posters concerning etymology, grammar, biology, geography, mathematics, geometry, social studies, and ethics. My two years of Montessori training made Pine Manor look like a piece of cake. To make money I worked three nights a week from midnight until 5 a.m. for the United Mine Workers Union. I filled out forms for the ill-fated people who had developed black lung disease. On my walk home at dawn I often had to leap to safety onto garden walls as packs of rats raced along the streets in a well-kept neighborhood of our nation's capital.

I slaved to maintain successful grades. It was a privilege to be taught by two protégées of Maria Montessori, Margaret E. Stephenson and Fahmida Malik, amongst other talented trainers. Since I took shorthand, I was able to record every syllable of their historical teaching sessions and copious demonstrations of manipulative materials. I spent every night transcribing my verbatim notes. Sometimes I had no time to sleep because we had to hand in our journals to be checked on the following day.

The Washington Montessori Institute's administrative staff requested copies of my notes for their files after inspecting my journals. Because of this honor I was able to barter with my classmates. I gave them pages of my approved work if they colored some of my timelines or created my math diagrams. I was grateful every day that I had learned how to type and take shorthand back in Cambridge.

I kidded my fellow students that I saved on water bills because I filled up my bathtub with my own tears. The curricular requirements were severe. One woman actually developed "hysterical cancer" due to the stress involved in the rigorous program. I always sat in the first row so I could be at the center of every class. This forced me to pay close attention to the lecturers. I recall becoming annoyed during one of Ms. Malik's lengthy talks because a comrade fell out of her seat and began rolling on the floor. She was having an anxiety attack. Not a soul assisted her because we were terrified to miss part of the instructional speech. Our weakened peer withdrew from the course the next day.

During my two years of training I also met Sanford Jones, another admired leader of the Montessori movement. He specialized in the areas of music and social studies. Mr. Jones was a part-time trainer and the full-time head of the world-renowned St. Michael's Montessori School on the Upper West Side of Manhattan. I was relieved to learn that the school rented its space from St. Michael's Church and was not religiously affiliated with it.

After two years I graduated from The Washington Montessori Institute with my Primary and Elementary international teaching degrees. My dream in life was to work at St. Michael's. I requested an interview with Mr. Jones and was hired. In the privacy of my apartment I collapsed onto my knees after he informed me of the excellent news over the phone. My diligence had paid off. I applied for and received my New York City and New York State teaching licenses. I proudly began my twenty-two year career at one of the finest schools in Manhattan.

# Chapter 7

## "Pose as his wife and everything will be fine."

Driving back and forth from Bronxville to Manhattan became wearisome and expensive. I can still recollect my astonishment when the disc jockey on my morning radio station cheerfully chirped, "The West Side Highway will be congested more than usual from now on due to construction which will take place over the NEXT FIVE YEARS!" I had to leave my car in a public garage every morning. It was a multi-leveled pitch black dungeon. Sometimes it was necessary to wait for up to thirty minutes while a good-natured drunken fellow with a funky red bandana around his neck and a dilapidated straw hat fetched my car. Everyone in line prayed that Cowboy wouldn't crash their car before delivering it to street level. We always heard tires screeching and couldn't help but imagine the worst. I knew that I had to find an apartment close to school as soon as possible or I would end up looking like <u>The Portrait of Dorian Gray</u> in drag by the end of the first semester.

I often worked seven days a week until 11 p.m. during the summer before school officially commenced. A Montessori environment is a very particular place. I designed the shelves and a talented father constructed and painted them. I ordered, unpacked, and arranged all of the child-sized furniture, manipulative materials, curtains, rugs, and examples of the five classes of vertebrates and their habitats. There was so much to prepare that the janitor found me on the floor passed out from exhaustion on quite a few occasions. My classroom was a showcase when the children and their folks arrived in early September.

I asked every parent and teacher if they knew of an apartment for rent. After school I explored hideous possibilities by myself. All of the rentals were ridiculously expensive minuscule studios. One place had no kitchen; just a hot plate in a closet. Another had a bed jammed into what was supposed to be a loft. If I had been a contortionist or part feline perhaps I could have occasionally napped when lack of sleep overcame me. An apartment that was actually decent had an enormous Jacuzzi which sounded like an outboard motor when I turned it on. The landlord look turned on too so I decided I'd be safer passing on that offer. A railroad apartment on Amsterdam Avenue right by my school was painted in such a bright shade of white that I would have been forced to wear sunglasses at all times. It was also so narrow that if I gained ten pounds, I wouldn't have been able to fit in my own living quarters. I was getting discouraged when an opportunity presented itself during a parent conference.

My first class of Montessori Primary students ranged from three to six years of age. It was a small but diverse group. There were children from Brazil, France, Israel, Japan, the Philippines, Poland, and of course, New York City. We got along very well and I was fortunate to have a terrific assistant. The only fly in the ointment was Sergio who was the largest, strongest, and oldest boy in the class. Sergio was an intelligent and street smart little guy who would have made St. Francis of Assisi harm small animals. He was hell on wheels. I needed him to be a leader but he was a dictator that would have given Stalin a run for his money.

My classroom was situated in the basement of St. Michael's Church which was an ideal location. There was a long hallway for the students' cubbies and belongings. We had our own private bathrooms and an extra empty room for musical and dramatic activities. The back door of the classroom led to a generous playground where there was a working garden, play equipment, and lots of room to run. One day after an especially disruptive morning with Sergio, I asked the assistant to take the other children to recess. I kept my impish charge with me. I sat him on a chair and informed him that I was the only boss in the room and that he better not forget it. I then made him remove all of the materials from the shelves with painstaking precision. Sergio scrubbed and dried each shelf before returning the dusted manipulatives to their exact positions. He swept the floors and halls, replaced the water in the flower vases, cleaned the animals' tanks, and polished the furniture. These chores took Sergio a full week to complete during class time and while the other children cheerfully played outside. I watched my rascal like a hawk.

When a dishpan-handed Sergio returned after a weekend of rest, he was a reformed individual. My former pain in the neck became my star student for the rest of the year. I called his mother for a conference to discuss the miraculous transformation. Carolina was a striking, sturdy, blonde, Argentinean mother of three. We roared when she told me that she was as tough as nails with Sergio at home. She congratulated me that I was intuitive enough to see that the only way to earn Sergio's respect was to demand it. I was on a pedestal in Sergio's mind now. His mom and I became fast friends for many years.

Carolina was in her mid-thirties and her Brazilian husband, Federico, was in his late sixties. He had been a handsome and popular race car driver who won her heart. They ran an import/export business downtown while her elderly mother took care of their children. Carolina explained that her mom was getting ready to return to Argentina because Sergio and his siblings were old enough to become latchkey kids. This was my lucky day because grandma's apartment was offered to me for an astounding $625 per month. I could stroll from my new pad to my classroom door in ten minutes. I hit the proverbial renters' jackpot.

There was one catch. I, like millions of other desperate Manhattanites, would be an illegal sublet. Therefore, I could not use my real name. I became Carolina II. Even if I had to pose as her for the rest of my life, Carolina's deal was too good to reject for a legal technicality. I didn't care if I ended up in prison. Later that week, Carolina and Federico gave me a tour of my prospective flat at night. The electricity was not turned on so Federico led me around while he lit a series of matches. His fingers were singed by the time I completed my inspection.

The inside of the place was a crap house but the building was safe, clean, and on Central Park West which is an excellent location due to its proximity to Central Park. The rental had a roomy kitchen, two deep closets, three dead bolt locks, and an alcove which were real bonuses in a city dwelling. There was a twenty-four hour concierge and parking galore. My one bedroom apartment was on the twentieth floor with a view that was to die for even in the dark. Best of all, the north wall was all windows. I was so high up that I could see the East River over the magnificent treetops of Central Park even though I was on the West Side of

New York City. In less than a week's time, I handed Carolina a wad of hundred dollar bills for the security payment and a few months' rent up front thanks to my charitable grandmother. I lived there for more than twenty years.

Claude and Claudine were teary eyed to see me depart from their nest once again because they knew I was leaving for good. Brief visits and holidays would bring us together in the future. They were honestly thrilled that I was starting my life in New York City with a respectable job in an honored profession and that I had landed a gem of an apartment. They couldn't wait for their first social call. I had a lot of work to do before I'd allow them to see my new home. My abode would be ready for a viewing by Christmas. It turned out that the timing of my departure from Bronxville was sadly apropos. The villa on the hill wasn't going to be in the family much longer due to my parents' dire financial straits. All of the Seiberts were going to have to find another place to live.

## "Just stand at the foot of the coffin."

It was exhilarating to experience the electricity which surged through my mind when I moved into my new residence. I became a human Con Edison plant. My motto for my apartment was, "I can't wait to renovate!" The first item flung into the garbage at the speed of light was a ghastly, rotating, mirrored, disco ball that was hanging in the middle of my living room. It made me nauseous when I flipped its switch and the room began to spin. The horribly stained moss green wall-to-wall carpet was a pleasure to slice up and drag to the incinerator room. To my amazement, gorgeous parquet floors hid beneath the grotesque rainbow speckled matting. I hired two maintenance men to paint the entire apartment in a neutral shade known as Navajo White.

Momps gave me carte blanche at a department store. I purchased almost everything I needed from two large imitation Oriental rugs to a polished wooden toilet seat. I hired a van, called a few friends, and loaded up any superfluous furniture and utensils that my mother and grandmother had on hand. An elegant dining room table which seated eight, Theresa's rocking chair, Milton's handsome desk, Portuguese marble topped chests of drawers, one claret leather club chair, two burgundy velvet club chairs, and an assortment of gilded mirrors, sconces, and knickknacks from my travels filled the vehicle to its capacity.

I was so enthralled with my flat that I decorated the place in a flash. Mom, dad, and Muffy came for their first visit on a crisp autumn day. The trees in Central Park simply took their breath away as they gazed out of my expansive windows. I knew that my folks approved of my mini-palace in the sky when ma stated, "We wouldn't be scared to live here."

My parents brought the "Seiberts' Special" traditional picnic lunch from the delicatessen in Bronxville. Mother and I always ordered turkey sandwiches but she never ate hers. She drank vodka as her beverage of choice and nibbled on a dill pickle. Father relished his roast beef sandwich with coleslaw and two glasses of ice cold milk. He was like a kid when it came to food. Dad also purchased any sort of giant cookie which was sold by the cash register as a highly caloric impulse buy. We shared that for dessert. Muffy ate the meat from ma's uneaten lunch and a Milk-Bone dog biscuit for a treat.

Dad watched a football game on TV and took a nap with the Muffster. Mom and I inspected my closet and chatted with my neighbors. In spite of the terrible phase my parents were going through as they prepared to move from their much loved home, they never let anything but a smile and supportive words cross their lips when they came to The Big Apple. We enjoyed a delightful afternoon each time they visited.

I didn't let on as to what I had discovered about my neighborhood. Every morning when I walked to work I passed PS 163 Alfred E. Smith School. Alfred was elected the forty-second Governor of New York four times. I chuckled because I knew his great-grandson from my youth at The Westchester Country Club. The past and present hotshots would have disapproved of how the students disrespected their namesakes' school property. I assumed that the kids threw miniature plastic containers on the street after classes each day. My feet made crunching sounds for a block as these tidbits were crushed beneath my high heels. I was so naïve that I didn't realize that they were really empty vials of crack.

I actually passed a dead body on the street but thank God that was a rarity. A few times I was pleased to see what I thought were street performers near Broadway. I guessed there was a mime school near my institution of learning. As the months passed, I was informed that when drug addicts are high out of their minds on heroin they stand in frozen poses for lengthy periods of time; so much for my guileless pantomime theory.

Mom and dad finally got their first clue about my dicey neighborhood at about 3 a.m. one week night. I received a call at 3:15 from a man who claimed he was a detective. He asked me to meet him on the corner of Central Park West and 97th Street. I told him that I didn't care if he was baby Jesus; I wouldn't dare go down to the street at that time unless he had some undeniable proof of who he was. The detective stated that he had just gotten off the phone with Claude. I hopped out of bed. It turned out that some madman with a baseball bat had smashed all the windows and mirrors of the cars on the street across from my building.

Fortunately, he was winded by the time he got to my Subaru. I only lost the glass on the driver's side. I had to sit on a pile of chards and find a garage that would take my car at 4 o'clock in the morning. Dad was less than pleased about the psychotic episode.

It became increasingly difficult to keep the idiosyncrasies of my 'hood from my parents especially when another detective called my mother a few months later. My wallet had been stolen during a stellar performance by comeback queen, Tina Turner, in an up close and personal little nightclub. I replaced my credit cards and driver's license and thought nothing more of the matter. The secretary at school summoned me from class one morning because mom was in a tizzy as to my whereabouts. An investigator had called ma and told her that her beloved daughter was high on cocaine and locked up in a jail cell in New Jersey after shoplifting and assaulting a police officer. My mother was her usual charming self and suggested that she was sure her Little Claudie was at school teaching the Montessori kiddies. I sheepishly explained to her that a hardened criminal had used my stolen identification and posed as me. The detective was infuriated because I decided not to press charges. I was afraid that my imposter would take revenge and beat the hell out of me when she was released from prison.

As the years passed, the Upper West Side became more and more gentrified. My parents received fewer calls. Crack vials and corpses disappeared from view. Now my old neighborhood is a sought after residential area. It's a shame that Momps never got to see my place as her health was failing. Neither did Federico.

Carolina's husband became ill and died within a few months after my move. The looming question in my mind was, "What the heck am I going to do since I was supposedly married to the guy?" Nothing could ruffle Carolina's feathers. She calmly stated, "Just stand at the foot of the coffin." Quite a few people attended Federico's wake. Carolina stood at the head of the casket and I took my position at the other end. I heard a few maintenance men mumbling something to the effect, "That lucky old bastard…."

My husband's wake dragged on for hours. There was a small herd of ancient, corpulent, professional mourners. Each one wailed louder than the other. The crying wasn't what bugged me. It was the fact that every hired griever recited an entire freaking rosary. I wanted to murder all of them and escape to the coast of Maine for a much needed vacation after standing at Federico's feet for what seemed like a lifetime. I thanked God that I never married.

## "You should never fall in love with a building."

Living with my parents in Bronxville for more than twenty years was similar to being a full time resident of Hollywood. Total illusion was the all-encompassing theme of their lives. Even their house started to fall apart as my dad tried unsuccessfully to rebuild his empire. God knows my father attempted to be the handyman he could no longer afford. Yet, bathtub caulking should never be used to fix cracks in the cement sidewalks of any home.

Mom and dad were still members of one of the most elite country clubs in the nation. However, they damn near froze to death in winter because there wasn't enough money to fill the gargantuan oil tank to heat the house. Priorities, anyone? Long gone was the sequoia of a Christmas tree. It was replaced by one of those awful artificial white ones which ma decorated with gold ornaments that weren't made of glass. A repugnant remnant of lamé was wrapped around its metal base. Only the original glowing angel on top of this Yuletide spectacle remained from passed holidays. She even looked depressed and out-of-place.

There were no presents to be found anywhere, anymore. Thank God my students were generous. I'd rewrap everything because Santa couldn't abandon Claude and Claudine. My mother truly grieved for the fact that she and dad were unable to provide me with an abundance of gifts. I honestly didn't care. Our holidays were once again intimate and meaningful without whirling hordes of partygoers. During one of the bleakest Christmases we ever shared, mom gave me her mother's exquisite diamond dinner ring. I sobbed with gratitude. Ma was not only loyal, she was generous too.

My parents still drove a lavender Cadillac with a white pleather roof. Unfortunately, they were driving the tires into the ground commuting to Hartford, Connecticut. Dad was forced to close the doors of his family's plant in New York City. Now, my folks had to personally proofread the newspaper, rent presses, and hire a skeleton crew to get the publication out on time. It was a four hour ride from Bronxville to Hartford and back. They left early in the morning and didn't return until late at night. Life for Claude and Claudine had turned into a vicious rat race thanks to the avarice of their closest relatives. To top it all off, The Internal Revenue Service audited my father and his bookkeeper embezzled him. It seemed like Lady Luck was forever kicking dad in the nuts.

In spite of everything, my parents partied on the weekends and desirable Claudine always looked like a million bucks. She cunningly bought cocktail dresses and gowns at Alexander's, Klein's, and Loehmann's where less expensive apparel was available. Ma purchased budget friendly high heels at Cross County Shopping Center in Yonkers and had them dyed to match her outfits. Sometimes she adorned her stilettos with marcasite or jeweled clasps which enhanced their appeal. None of these tricks tarnished my mother's fashionable reputation because she had a unique sense of style that couldn't be equaled. Mom designed many of her clothes and had tailors from less wealthy communities make her remarkable outfits. She travelled to those same areas and found outrageous costume jewelry for pennies.

My mother was ingenious in many ways. She could have been a successful fashion designer. I have a portfolio of her creations that's three inches thick. Ma used India ink and luscious watercolors to depict her extensive collection. Sadly, her parents wouldn't allow her to mingle with the "lowly types" who populated the Fashion District in New York City. Mom's potentially fulfilling career was terminated before it began.

Dad's history was similar in the sense that his dreams were also thwarted by his wayward relatives. My father yearned to be a doctor and had acquired knowledge and experience as a pharmacist in The United States Merchant Marine. He was born to two highly dysfunctional individuals who were seriously wealthy. Regrettably, his father was a compulsive gambler who lost the family's Scarsdale, New York estate at the race track. Dad stepped in to save the day and supported his parents until their deaths. He ran his family's financial newspaper, employed his brother and aunts, and helped out his sister on numerous occasions. He was successful until his in-laws stabbed him in the back.

Before my folks' daily venture to Hartford, dad made frequent pit stops at my maternal grandmother's apartment. He rightfully asked for money to keep his devastated newspaper afloat for a few more months and to pay some bills. Momps handed over a series of substantial checks but eventually refused to "burn money any more" even though she and her deceased husband had caused the entire dilemma. Dad was worn out by this time and unknowingly sold the remains of his business to a charlatan and agreed to stay on as a consultant. The only thing dad got out of that deal was a lengthy lawsuit. My father never collected a dime and was forced to make the heartbreaking decision to sell my mother's favorite possession in the world, her beautiful villa on the hill. A wise neighbor, who had been a dear friend for years, gave her advice which she completely ignored, "Claudine, you should never fall in love with a building." Regrettably, she had; lock, stock, and barrel. Consequently, that lovely lady's downfall was set in motion.

## "Thank God she died with her rice pudding recipe!"

Lady Luck had done a number on Claude for years. Now, Claudine was her primary focus of attention. Mom stood by her man through thick, thin, and thinner. Knowing she had to leave her heavenly home was bad enough but losing her mother was a severe blow. It didn't matter how ma's parents abused her pint-size family; she never stopped loving Momps and Pops.

My maternal grandmother was a Scorpionic, creative, and statuesque woman who dressed with style. Theresa was also one of the best cooks in town. She was the type of talented chef who didn't measure anything and intuited how to mastermind meals that made grown men drool. Even the nuns at my schools begged Momps to make her famous cherry cheese cake for their bake sales. Families forked over big bucks for that delectable indulgence. Of course, she made extras for the sisters, priests, and monsignors. Thank God Momps died with her rice pudding recipe. Half of Westchester County would be a great deal chubbier if that original dessert still existed.

Grandma was blue eyed, fair-skinned, and had long silver hair streaked with dark brown at the nape of her neck which she swept up in a French knot. After Pops' demise, Momps dated a string of men who died after a few years of courting her. Each old timer asked for her hand in marriage but she declined. Her standard response to a proposal was, "No thanks. I'm never going to roll around another bag of bones in a wheel chair after what I went through with Milt."

My mother waited on my grandmother hand and foot. Ma made sure Momps' social calendar was chocked full of engagements even if it meant she tagged along to bridge luncheons. Momps was a competitive and talented bridge player. These afternoon games included quite a few drinkies which continued when the hubbies joined the gals after the early evening trains arrived from New York City. She gladly joined in on the fun and often went shopping or dined with my mother's friends without my mother.

My grandmother was independent and fit until the last two years of her life. She put my mom through the ringer when her health began to fade. In delirious states after hip surgeries in Bronxville's Lawrence Hospital, Momps repeatedly whispered to my mother that she wished mom had died instead of her older sister. In spite of this taunting, ma hired round-the-clock nurses so my grandma was never alone. Theresa Kennedy died at the age of ninety-one of congestive heart failure. Ma sold the majority of the contents of my grandparents' splendid apartment as fast as she could. The capital allowed my folks to hang on until they figured out the next strategic move in their lives which had become a game of survival.

I loved my grandmother dearly but was cognizant of the fact that everything she gave me was purchased with dad's blood money. Momps took excellent care of me for years with my father's funds. Without her financial backing, I would not have been blessed with an exceptional education, decent clothes, furnishings for my apartments, birthday and holiday cash, or cars. I never felt guilty for accepting her generosity. I figured it was my birthright that simply took an alternate route.

# "Please take these grapefruits; I'm off to Alaska."

There was a void in my life after Momps died. I needed a grandmother to confide in and someone who would love me unconditionally. Mothers are too close. Somebody else's grandma is perfection. There's nothing like skipping a generation because the all-encompassing need to control gene is generally absent in older folks. My neighbor, Christine Cooper, fit the bill.

I am an outgoing individual and greeted practically everyone at my apartment house in Manhattan with a smile and a few kind words. I never bothered to ask names. Consequently, conversations cropped up on the sidewalk, mail room, elevator, and hallways at all hours of the day and night. I became friends with many of my neighbors in spite of not knowing their monikers. They discussed various events in their lives and facts concerning their medical and personal problems without hesitation. People often told me their darkest secrets within a few minutes of our meeting.

I must have met Christine a hundred times when we fetched our mail. She was always dressed immaculately. Her hair and make-up were impeccable. Hell, Mrs. Cooper looked better than I did most of the time and she was ninety years old. Christine walked with a cane because her knees were arthritic. We'd amble to the elevator and chat until we reached her floor. It was a pleasure each time our paths crossed.

The day after school ended in June, I'd be off on some adventure. A few days before my scheduled departure for Washington state and Alaska, I received a carton of Harry & David's scrumptious sweet pink grapefruits. There was no way I could consume them so I offered the citrus delicacies to Christine. She gratefully accepted my gift and I delivered them to her apartment.

We had developed a bond before the exchange so it seemed comical that we had never formally introduced ourselves. Mrs. Cooper asked my name and apartment number because she wanted to send me a thank you note. She was entranced by the fact that I was venturing to Alaska by myself. Christine commented that she had a little something for me upon my arrival home and to please contact her at my convenience. I remember this day so clearly. Mrs. Cooper was wearing a pale peach cotton suit and spotless beige orthopedic shoes. Her cheeks and lip color were coordinated with her outfit. Christine's gray eyes matched her hair. I looked forward to seeing her again and sharing the tales of my journey.

The concierge handed me two letters and a package when I returned from my glacial expedition. He told me that Christine's granddaughter had left the articles for me. Mrs. Cooper had moved into a nursing home because she had suffered a stroke. I unpacked with a sense of dread. I was afraid to read the notes and to discover what was in the parcel. The message from Christine's relative contained the address of the rehabilitation center where my elderly pal now dwelled. The other envelope contained Mrs. Cooper's promised thank you note and an explanation of her fascination with Alaska.

This marvelous woman was one of the first registered nurses who cared for Inuits that were stricken with tuberculosis of the spine. Decades earlier, Christine created a life for herself as a caretaker in the wilderness. She ventured where the grizzliest of men dared not go. Here was a woman I truly admired. The package contained handmade gifts from her patients which she bestowed upon me. There was a sealskin thimble, stationery with hand painted Eskimo children in various poses, a delicate white cotton handkerchief with the map of Alaska outlined and labeled in colorful thread on its surface, a bone carving of a caribou in water up to its knees with two hungry wolves at its heels, a fringed colorful table cloth with the names of some of Christine's patients written in assorted inks, and a pair of painted leather clip-on earrings trimmed in white fur which depicted two small round heads of smiling Inuit women. I reverently shared Mrs. Cooper's mementos with my students for years.

I tracked down Christine the next day. Luckily, she wasn't far away. Her new address on 87th Street and West End Avenue was a stone's throw from Riverside Park and the Hudson River. I visited her a few times a week after work or after my flat and jumping lessons at the historic Claremont Riding Academy which was located on 89th Street. On the weekends and on holidays, I'd call on her after I rode.

The week before Thanksgiving a van full of residents from her home were driven to my school for a feast. My Thanksgiving Day tradition was to go for an early ride in the park and pick up two delicious turkey meals with all the trimmings from a diner on Broadway. Christine and I enjoyed a delectable lunch together. She introduced me to the tasty sensation known as sweet potato pie. I'd then ingest a few Rolaids and travel to my parents for dinner.

Christine and I sat and talked for hours whenever we got together. I'd tell her everything that was going on in my life. The woman never winced and offered sagacious advice when asked for it. Mrs. Cooper was incredibly open-minded and full of plain old common sense and thought-provoking anecdotes. She also reminisced about what it was like to live in Manhattan in the early 1900's. Christine harked back to winters when she and her chums sledded down Broadway for miles without the need to halt for traffic. She explained how children played freely on the city sidewalks until elderly lamplighters came with their ladders to manually ignite the gas streetlights. That was the signal for all the kids to rush home.

Mrs. Cooper told the story behind every keepsake she received from her Inuit patients. She also described what it was like to live as a single woman in Alaska. Christine was a handsome lady whose heritage was mesmerizing. Her descendants were Native American, African American, and Caucasian. Our photograph sits on my grandfather's desk in my den in Florida. People comment that I "closely resemble my grandmother." That observation is uncannily correct.

When the weather was warm, I rolled Mrs. Cooper's wheelchair to Riverside Park for a picnic. I read to her when her eyes no longer functioned well enough to do so. She requested that I write about her life. Christine dictated how her strict father had forced her to learn to ride even though she was deathly afraid of horses. She never forgave him for lessons which promoted the development of her courage.

Mrs. Cooper had a younger brother. She loved him dearly and was saddened by the fact that he lived in a special home. He could not fend for himself because of "problems with his nerves." Christine showed me his photograph. He looked like Marvin Gaye.

Her mother was an excellent cook who died in her thirties. Mrs. Cooper was informed that her mom wasted away from "serious female issues." Christine was married three times and outlived all of her husbands. She gave birth to one daughter who succumbed to ovarian cancer at an early age. Mrs. Cooper found it hard to discuss the loss of her only child.

Christine described herself as a "vain and callous woman" who "loved the good life." That is precisely why she decided to "change her ways" and "devote" herself to "sick and helpless people that no one cared about." We didn't pursue her biography beyond those basic facts. She decided that writing a memoir was just too painful. I appreciated her point of view.

I refuse to believe that Mrs. Cooper was anything except the angel I came to cherish. We had an incomparable rapport for more than a decade. Her deepest desire was to celebrate her one hundredth birthday. Christine died a couple of months before she reached the tender age of one hundred one. I think of her every day and still miss her company. In retrospect, our relationship was valuable preparation for what destiny had planned for my family.

# Chapter 8

## "We want to go to Cairo instead of Orlando."

After a year in the basement with the Primary children at St. Michael's Montessori School, The Board of Trustees asked if I'd care to teach at the Elementary Level. The spacious top floor of the school consisted of one classroom of thirty-six first to third graders and another connecting classroom of about twenty to thirty fourth to sixth graders. The Board specifically wanted me to instruct the older group of children. I thought that would be too much of a jump for a novice such as myself and respectfully declined. They were furious. Plus, they did not offer an increase in salary for a much more demanding position. My parents thought I was nuts to jeopardize my new job. I held out, got the bucks, and obtained the appointment I wanted as the Lower Elementary level instructor. That meant I moved upstairs.

St. Michael's Church and the facades of its connecting buildings are spectacular. The Church has the finest collection of Tiffany windows in New York City. My students could view these works of art from their seats. Everyone had to climb the wide, black, polished stone steps of a tower to reach the enormous Elementary classrooms. This prodigious learning center had terrazzo floors, twenty foot domed ceilings, extensive windows, a loft, a small stage, two double bathrooms, six sinks, a library, and every handmade Montessori material known to mankind.

My folks were given a grand tour by my principal. They were duly impressed and showed their appreciation by taking us to lunch. Dad splurged in celebration of my coup. He escorted my mom, my boss, my assistant, another teacher, and me to dine at Tavern on the Green, a swanky landmark restaurant in Central Park. It was a swell day.

I soon discovered that the vast majority of mothers and fathers of New York City private school pupils are exceptionally demanding. They give a new and deeper meaning to the word hovering. I also realized that the primary and elementary academic force spent more time with its students than the parents did. It didn't take long after those eureka moments for me to thank God that teachers are afforded several breaks throughout the year and lengthy summer vacations. We need that time to refuel or we'd burn out in a couple of years. Still, teaching is an enormously rewarding occupation especially if you had a classroom like mine.

Momps purchased my automobile so I didn't have a car payment each month. Carolina's rent for my flat on Central Park West was absurdly low. Therefore, I was able to save money without skimping on my social life. I began to take advantage of my vacation time. A thoughtful and knowledgeable agent was recommended to me. Eileen was responsible for igniting my passion for national and international travel. At work I became known for sharing adventurous stories with my students when teachable moments arose during the school day. Parents kidded me that they were upset because their kids would whine, "We want to go to Cairo instead of Orlando!"

When Momps passed away, I inherited a modest chunk of change and immediately booked a ticket to Egypt. My mother convinced herself that I would be kidnapped and sold into slavery. Dad wished he could steal away in my suitcase. The State Department contacted me on numerous occasions before my departure. I was strongly advised to cancel my plans because I "was endangering my life." I was scheduled to leave at the height of The Persian Gulf War. I figured Egypt would either be one of the safest or most dangerous places on Earth. It turned out to be the trip of a lifetime. There were no tourists in the whole country except for me, two Germans, and a Spanish family.

I always travel by myself but have tour guides, drivers, hotels, bed and breakfasts, museums, side trips, and boat, airplane, and helicopter excursions booked in advance. I give my travel agent a general idea of what I want to see and have her fill in the blanks with what average tourists don't experience. Eileen also sets me up with local residents that she's made friends with during her expeditions. These preparations allow for spontaneity but give me the opportunity to more fully experience a foreign culture.

It was a long and exhausting trip to Egypt because of the overlay in London. I was ecstatic that British Airways made a booking error and bumped me up to first class. I thanked the gods and goddesses as I walked upstairs to my roomy seat with a mere half a dozen people as flying companions. It was glorious not being cramped in coach. Every time I applied lipstick and readied myself to land, another Clint Eastwood movie would appear on our private screen. I looked like Ramses II in drag by the time we arrived.

It was strangely exciting to be greeted by eager young soldiers aiming Uzi machine guns at my frontal cortex as I dragged my weary limbs through the airport in Cairo. I found it amusing that I received many smiles and an occasional sigh of lustful appreciation from the military men due to my dark hair and eyes. However, their itchy trigger fingers were ready to blow out my brains if I made one false move.

I could view the pyramids of Giza from my hotel room. Eileen wisely arranged for a married female physician to be my guide. This delightful Egyptian citizen earned extra income by escorting tourists around Cairo and its surrounding areas. Our driver didn't speak a word of English. His enormous muscles, stern expression, and masterful driving skills behind the wheel of a black Mercedes sedan were the precise elements necessary for a safe and carefree stay in the Land of the Nile.

My initial request was to visit The Step Pyramid of Pharaoh Djoser which is the world's first pyramid. The complex is less than ten miles south of Cairo in Saqqara. Only one guard was present to protect the 210 foot tall masterpiece. I was in awe and could positively feel history pulsating around us. The sentry gestured for us to enter a small gated tomb. My guide stated that this was an extraordinary treat. We hunched over and entered a sacred site complete with half buried skulls and bones in the sand. To my horror, the jokester of a sentinel picked up what appeared to be the cranium of a child and tossed it to me. I caught it and feared that Osiris himself would strike us dead for such foolishness. I gently handed the miniature noggin to my chaperone with an expression in my eyes which screamed, "Let's get the heck out of here!"

I spent the ensuing week on the Nile drifting through time until my boat reached the Aswan Dam. I frequently disembarked for small side trips. One of my favorite detours was to a sculptor's studio who worked in alabaster. The artist found it perplexing that I asked to keep a magnificent discarded chunk of gypsum that was the size of an apple. It bore his chisel marks. I purchased a small vase in appreciation but still cherish my work in process which had been delegated to a garbage heap.

My skin felt as if it was on fire when I stepped into the sun in the revered Theban necropolis of the Valley of the Kings and Queens. I bolted to a merchant to purchase a lengthy white cotton shawl to cover myself. The dry air and burning ultra-violet rays would make anyone look like Tutankamun's mummy in no time at all.

My final days in Egypt were spent flying to investigate the two massive rock temples in Nubia called Abu Simbel and absorbing the spectacular exhibits at the museum in Cairo. I bought over a hundred postcards, slides, books, scarabs, scrolls of papyrus, and other artifacts for my students with the hope that I would spark a similar desire to travel in their young hearts.

When I returned to New York City, I visited the impressive Metropolitan Museum of Art's ancient Egyptian exhibits every chance I got. I also attended classes at the Met and took notes concerning numerous topics from how to make papyrus and beer to the afterlife. After weeks of preparation, I made reservations at The Metropolitan for a grand tour for my students. I also scouted out a nearby playground on Fifth Avenue where we could eat lunch and play after our studies. We travelled by public bus and politely strolled through the grand hallways as I discussed aspects of ancient Egyptian life. The outing was an educational victory. My class of six to nine year olds begged for more knowledge. They devoured any information they could obtain on Egyptian culture, mythology, history, geography, and geometry. We returned three more times to investigate the distant civilizations of Mesopotamia, Greece, and Rome.

Within a few months of my return from North Africa, the children began bringing their deceased small animals to school. The kids felt their pets would be more happily ensconced in the underworld if we conducted a ceremony resembling the ancients. I treasure the memory of a little girl and her lifeless hamster which she transported in a shoebox. One morning she entered class with an elaborately painted cardboard coffin. It was painstakingly decorated to look like a sarcophagus and even included the symbol of the Eye of Horus. Unprompted, an older boy picked up a copy of my Book of the Dead and began reading passages as all of the children, one by one, became quiet as mice. They bent their heads in respect for the dearly departed mammal. After lunch we peacefully processed to Central Park and buried Hammy, the rodent.

Other children preferred that we place a coin in the casket of their fish, amphibian, reptile, bird, or mammal. They favored the olden Greek custom of paying a toll before crossing the river Styx in order to enter the world of the afterlife. Parents called and thanked me because there were no more hysterics when a pet died. The pupils knew that they could come to Ms. Seibert's classroom and a short ceremony would be performed with a few well-chosen buddies. Everyone involved felt that a natural cycle had been completed. It was also understood by the students that a healthy time period should elapse before another pet was purchased in deference to the deceased. They gave serious consideration before embarking on another important relationship with an animal. This was an important lesson for the children in our consumer driven society.

My journey to Egypt was significant on many levels. My reputation grew as the teacher who possessed an unbridled enthusiasm for travel, studying ancient civilizations, and riding horses. To the astonishment of their family members, youngsters in my class often discussed facts at the dinner table relating to cuneiform or Sumerian wedge-shaped writing, Roman frescos, and how to safely clean the frog of a hoof. Of course, my students completed the New York State curriculum but that was covered quickly and efficiently. In a Montessori class there is the freedom to follow the children's interests and delve deeply into subject matter using hands-on materials. My adoration of the never-ending cycle of learning was nourished every day at work. I couldn't have asked for a more fulfilling occupation.

# "Dudley Moore is at the back door!"

My adoration of the never-ending cycle of learning did not include any postgraduate studies. I was sorely disappointed to learn that it is mandatory for all elementary school teachers to obtain a Master of Arts in Education. Once again, it was Momps' funds which paid for my schooling at Columbia University in Manhattan. I skipped two consecutive summers of travel in order to cram in as many credits as possible during back-to-back sessions of courses. My skin was blanched by the time my teaching responsibilities resumed in September.

I was astounded that the students at St. Michael's were eager to commence their studies in the fall. Mondays were always the best day of the week because the children actually missed the camaraderie of learning after a weekend of play and relaxation. Their parents were also enthusiastic to comprehend the philosophy of The Montessori Method so, all of the instructors spent hours preparing workshops for family members. Timelines, grammar boxes for learning parts of speech, small moveable alphabets in different colors for word studies, botany material, geometry equipment, social studies cards and pictures, wooden puzzle maps of the continents, science experiments, and agendas of spectacular field trips and guest speakers were meticulously set up in every classroom so we could demonstrate and explain the program in an uncomplicated yet riveting manner.

I lectured for a minimum of an hour and spent another sixty minutes answering questions. The process of educating parents occurred at various times throughout the year. Family members and teachers exited from the classrooms with a sense of satisfaction knowing that the young citizens of tomorrow were following their interests in a school which fostered a love of learning not rote memorization of facts.

I always locked the back door of my classroom so parents were forced to climb the stairs of the tower after enjoying refreshments in the lobby. This way I could greet each person as they strolled through the main entrance. On one of many memorable evenings the room was crowded with inquisitive folks. I was ready to begin my presentation when I heard a loud pounding at the rear of the room. I looked through the small glass window of the white metal fire door but couldn't see anybody in the dark hallway. I turned and took a few steps. The banging resumed. I was a bit peeved at that point so I unbolted the door and swung it open with a frown on my face. I imagined that a mischievous child was playing a trick on me. To my surprise, a grinning Dudley Moore, the talented actor and musician, stood at the threshold. He seductively glanced at me from head to toe and stated that he wished I had been his teacher. We both laughed as I led him to a seat next to his wife at the time, Tuesday Weld. I began the evening with a sensational science experiment involving a propane tank and immediately scorched my fingers. Everyone oohed and aahed as I wondered if paramedics could make it up the stairs in time to save my left hand. The evening was a success. No one ever discovered that I had cooked part of a limb.

One of the most admirable aspects of St. Michael's was that the kids of the rich and famous studied side by side with children whose parent(s) struggled to pay the rent. The well-to-do families donated money to a fund which enabled less fortunate individuals to send their offspring to our school. The Board of Trustees was also proud that our tuition was one of the lowest in the Metropolitan area.

After I completed my master's degree at Columbia, I began travelling during our two week winter and spring vacations to rejuvenate my brain cells and to beef up my social studies units. My admiration of pyramids and fascination with caves led me to explore Mexico in March for a few years. The Teotihuacan Pyramids near Mexico City whet my appetite for Chichen Itza, the most famous and best restored Mayan pyramid complex of the Yucatan Peninsula. I yearned to see more ancient sites so I decided to fly to Merida to view the amazing pyramid at Uxmal.

When I was at the Cancun airport, I was approached by an intoxicated young married couple from the Midwest. They inquired if I spoke English. I retorted in an extra thick Brooklyn accent, "Yeah, what da hell do yous want?" They guffawed and asked a series of mundane questions. I couldn't help but notice that the husband was missing a thumb. During the course of our stunted conversation, he mentioned some hideous farming accident. I wished them well and boarded my flight.

When I arrived in Merida I took a cab to my hotel. It appeared that my driver wasn't related to Son of Sam so I hired him to take me to Uxmal and the nearby caves. I noticed with some consternation that my friendly chauffeur was also missing a thumb. He was amazed that I boldly asked him why one of his major digits was no longer present. I was informed that it was lost in a childhood mishap. I told him about my thumbless acquaintance at the airport. I extracted a solemn vow that he would return me to the airport with both my thumbs intact. The driver laughed and complied with my wish. I thoroughly enjoyed my fascinating adventure visiting the quaint city of Merida, Uxmal, and the caverns. Plus, there is a fabulous gift store at the pyramid site. I am always on the lookout for captivating artifacts for my classroom. I found a pocketbook that was made out of a frog. Its stomach had a zipper in it. I knew this was a horrifying misuse of an animal but I justified buying it because it was an excellent specimen of an amphibian for the children to examine. I also purchased a unique three foot long, yellow, orange, red, white, and black painted snake sculpture which was carved out of a serpentine shaped root. Upon my return, I placed my souvenirs on a desk in my quarters and went to dinner. After my meal, I was puzzled why my room hadn't been tidied up and called the front desk. I was told that the chamber maid had been startled by my purchases and no longer wished to visit my room. Rumor had it that I was some sort of sorceress. Come to think of it, I did notice quite a few startled faces as I walked through the airports on my way home to New York with my colorful asp in hand.

My trips to Mexico and Egypt were the first of many unforgettable journeys that led me to travel across five continents. Year after year I returned refreshed and inspired with my arms filled with treasures from mysterious places and outlandish stories to thrill my youthful audiences. I'm pleased to report that to this day I possess both of my thumbs and students still handle that poor frog with the greatest of care.

# "We've been together for over thirty years; now get the hell out!"

St. Michael's Montessori School was founded in the 1960's as a parents' cooperative and rented its space from St. Michael's Church. The school was internationally respected for its vibrant and creative faculty and its adherence to Dr. Maria Montessori's philosophy. My colleagues and I had the honor of meeting Mario Montessori, Maria's son, when he visited St. Michael's shortly after I began my position as a Lower Elementary guide. Educators from around the world came to visit the classrooms throughout the year. Students were so involved with their lessons that onlookers and parent observers didn't faze them in the least. One afternoon more than a dozen Japanese male teachers came to tour our haven. Each gentleman wore a brown suit, a monochromatic tie, and had a camera hanging around his neck. I even became a bit rattled as they respectfully tiptoed around the environment. If a child happened to look up, he/she simply smiled and continued working. SMMS was an academic paradise.

Our school was a thriving, highly regarded, sparkling clean, and enchanting institution of learning which served a few hundred children between the ages of three and twelve. The Board continually improved the floors we leased for over three decades. In 1996 the school moved to 85th Street and West End Avenue not because we wanted to but because we were forced to do so. It was a tremendous shock when the greedy administrators of the Church told us that they were not renewing our lease and that we had to evacuate the premises when the school year ended. They planned on expanding but were not able to find another tenant. St. Michael's Church not only shot itself in the foot but ended up amputating one of its legs.

Parents scrambled to find another suitable site. They canvassed the surrounding neighborhood and miraculously located a building with an adjacent lot which used to be Randolph Hearst's old carriage house and stable yard. The Board negotiated a lease and construction continued at an animated pace throughout the summer. Before the children left for vacation in June, every student and their teachers along with the entire faculty and many parents walked in a procession to our new home, Metropolitan Montessori School. The adults felt that it would be an easier transition in September if the pupils actually saw that they had a place to continue their education even if it was in the process of being built. MMS purchased the building by 2009.

I was grateful to have a job after being thrown out of my classroom by the clergy. However, packing was a nerve racking experience. I had enough materials and books for a small country. My new classroom was a fourth of the size of my original palace. Talk about downsizing. It was like teaching with a girdle on my brain.

Management began cracking down on illegal sublets all over the city while I was adjusting to my new working conditions. The thought of living with Claude and Claudine again never entered my mind. After all, they were going to be homeless soon if an act of God didn't befall them. Out of the blue, I received a generous bonus from the school Board for my twentieth anniversary of teaching. I knew that my charade of posing as Carolina's double was coming to an end. I had also matured enough to realize that renting an apartment was not fiscally sound. Why not actually own a smidgen of real estate in Manhattan? My windfall promptly became the down payment for my very own one bedroom apartment which was only twelve blocks north of my longtime rental. I purchased the place with the assistance of a real estate magnate whose children I taught. I moved during a blizzard and began the next phase of my life as a homeowner.

My parents never saw my new apartment in person. They were hogtied by their problems. I also believe that Claude and Claudine were taken aback by the fact that I hadn't asked for their advice in the matter. Nevertheless, it was easy to get the place in order because it is relatively roomy and has lots of closets. There is even a room in the basement for bicycles, a storage area for each tenant, a gym, a laundry room, a roof deck for barbecues and lounging, and a recreational facility for meetings and parties. To my delight, there are four plots for plants at the front of the building. I became an enthusiastic gardener on the Upper West Side of Manhattan.

Two stately oak trees stand across from the entrance. There is a square bed of soil at the base of each trunk which is surrounded by six inch high black metal arches. In addition, there are two raised areas which measure approximately six feet by nine feet on either side of the lobby door. A three foot high fence of wrought iron spires surrounds each plot. I had to climb a ladder and carefully maneuver myself over these deadly ornamentations in order to achieve my botanical visions.

It took ages to clean the crap out of the soil and prepare it for new life. You name it; I found it. There were innumerable wads of rock hard gum, a watch, broken sunglasses, religious literature, hypodermic needles, close to ten dollars in filthy change, empty buried beer bottles, and about five hundred cigarette butts. I planted miniature pine trees, various bushes, ivy, and oodles of impatiens. We finally had curb appeal.

I also went riding in Central Park on the weekends after gardening. Precipitation didn't prevent me from hopping on a horse. The canopies of trees acted like giant umbrellas and the visor on my helmet prevented most of my face from getting wet. Another advantage to riding in the rain was that the moronic mothers who pushed their baby carriages on the bridle path were absent.

I often walked home from the stables in a euphoric state. Early one morning as I turned the corner onto my block, I squinted to obtain a better view of what appeared to be a blackened sidewalk in front of my home. Some fiend had risked castration on metal spikes to extract my blooming impatiens. The trustees authorized the purchase of more flowers and I managed to get some donated from a neighborhood association. However, plant after plant continued to be stolen. I became disheartened.

The Board finally decided that it would no longer finance the efforts of a serial abductor of the choicest blossoms and shrubs in the 'hood. My atypical urban hobby came to a grinding halt. I imagined a dirt stained mongrel with a flower fetish that lived as a recluse in a nearby apartment. I pictured he'd clean up on Sundays and deliver my stolen beauties to his adoring and unsuspecting mother. Fortunately, I had taken dozens of photographs of my gardening endeavors in full bloom including the exterior of the building and a shot from every possible angle of the interior of my apartment and its furnishings for my parents to admire in absentia.

As much as I relished the sense of accomplishment which accompanied the purchase of my abode, I sorely missed the open and expansive views of Central Park throughout the seasons. I felt like I was vacationing in a rabbit hole at my new pad. It never truly felt like home. It seemed as if I was in a state of flux after nearly two decades of relative stability. My school had relocated. I abandoned one of the choicest apartments in New York City and my parents were practically destitute.

I'll never forget the odd experience I had when I stepped out of my car on a wintry afternoon. My damp riding boot hovered for a few seconds before it touched Broadway. I stared at my leather encased foot for a moment. It appeared as if it wasn't connected to my body. A strange feeling came over me. I was enveloped by the thought that I wasn't going to be in Manhattan much longer. My notion left me in a daze.

About a month later, I received a job offer. At first it seemed like a scandalous scheme to leave Metropolitan Montessori School. I had considered myself to be a loyal lifer. I mentally scanned my career in New York City. I had taught for sixteen years at SMMS and six at MMS. I had survived six administrators. To everyone's surprise including my own, I defected to an outstanding Montessori school in Wilton, Connecticut. I decided to work for a visionary of an administrator who had been my former employer. It seemed like a breath of country air and another magnificent classroom were just what I needed. Little did I know that Claude and Claudine were hot on my heels.

# Part II: "Good Lord, it's happening to me."
## Chapter 9

### "They're going to fill in the swimming pool?"

My folks were desperate. The money from selling my grandparents' possessions was running low. It was unadulterated madness that Pops and Momps had rented their apartment in Bronxville for over fifty years. My father would have been on Easy Street if he had the opportunity to sell that place. Dad could have paid off his debts and saved the house. Instead, he had to mortgage and re-mortgage our home. To make things worse, the real estate market was tanking. Dad finally found interested buyers after radically reducing the price of the villa. My parents had to evacuate quickly. Fortuitously, dad got wind of a spacious and appealing apartment with a large terrace in Greenwich, Connecticut. An acquaintance of a friend had to place his sickly mother in a retirement home and wanted to sell her apartment expediently. Voila! Claude and Claudine had a new and reasonably priced home in an exclusive area. Now all they had to do was downsize, pack, and move forty years of belongings in six weeks' time.

A room of spectacular wrought iron furniture left behind after the big move.

During the weekend before the big day, dad literally gave away a ton of our possessions to neighbors and grateful passersby. You name it and my father gladly distributed it free of charge: a huge piano that had been a birthday gift to me, beds, headboards, ancient gardening equipment, printing paraphernalia, folding chairs and tables from memorable gatherings, large cut glass flower vases in various shapes and sizes that were used at parties to decorate the grounds, black and chrome torches which lit the property during nighttime festivities, loads of white garden furniture, pots of blooming flowers, a spinning wheel, ironing boards, dress racks full of clothes, and countless pairs of shoes.

The actual day of the move left my mother numb and paralyzed. She sat wrapped in a pale yellow sheet on their four poster bed and stared confusedly at the green flowered Oriental rug beneath her feet. Movers respectfully ignored her as they carted away the antique wooden night stands. My parents were so debilitated by this lightning quick departure from their revered home that they stayed at a Holiday Inn in Connecticut for weeks before venturing to their new abode.

Claude, Claudine, and Muffy II finally made their way to their Greenwich apartment which was crammed to the ceiling with cartons and enough furniture to fill a sizeable house. Mom crawled into their king size bed and never really got out of it again. Dad became friendly with the superintendent and his associates in order to make the place livable. My father did everything in his power to make my mother comfortable but she despised the place. At Christmas he lugged a six foot unpretentious fresh pine tree through the living room and onto the patio. He strung sparkling white lights on it to please her. It didn't work. Ma was broken in a sense and her health began to deteriorate.

It got to the point where she could hardly walk due to a painful hip condition. My mother also developed an ailment that made it difficult to swallow solids. No matter how she felt, dad dragged her out to lunch and dinner. She consumed numerous martinis as a meal. In spite of it all, my parents became popular residents of Greenwich and were greeted with open arms at cocktail parties, local restaurants, and hairdressers for seven years. Mom was weak but still charming and beautiful. Dad was the most devoted husband on the block.

Friends from the old neighborhood kept in touch with my folks. Gossip about how the new owners redecorated or repainted our house was the number one topic of discussion. My mother almost fainted when she received the report that those fools had demolished her treasured fountain and spiral black wrought iron staircase, ripped out the custom built doors of the breakfast room, relocated the kitchen to the living room, painted the house the color of mustard, and horror of all horrors, filled in the swimming pool and transformed it into a garden. My mother took to her bed for weeks.

## "The State Police are after us!"

The roles were reversed. Now, it was dad's turn. Claude took care of Claudine in Connecticut. Mom's attire slowly transmuted from pastel knit suits paired with sensible two inch heels to comfortable velveteen slacks and long-sleeved tops coupled with black patent leather flats to brightly colored caftans and gold slippers. Her bright red lipstick softened to a fuchsia glow and her platinum blond hair was white. Ma's Venus de Milo figure metamorphosed into a slender and delicate form. Regardless of her condition, mom still wore sparkling diamond rings and fancy gold or pearl earrings. She daintily sipped her constant companion, a pain killing tumbler of iced vodka. Her intake of food dwindled to that of a bird's. For the better part of the day, my mother remained in bed propped up by fluffy pillows and read <u>Women's Wear Daily</u>, <u>Vogue</u>, and <u>W Magazine</u>.

My father wore a uniform consisting of an Izod shirt, black loafers, a sports jacket, and black, brown or beige polyester pants as he broke his ass cleaning, shopping, and providing entertainment for mom. He arranged small dinner parties and modest holiday get-togethers and willingly prepared and served canapés and festive meals. Dad was visibly relieved to be unshackled from his sickly relatives, blood sucking newspaper, and money pit of a house. My parents finally had a few bucks again and splurged on occasion. They purchased another bundle of poodle joy, Muffy III. My father bought a long dreamed of toy, a twenty-six foot second hand Bayliner cruiser, and mom got a face-lift. After her swelling went down, I even felt younger. She looked gorgeous as her baby blue eyes gained prominence once more. It was the best plastic surgery I've ever seen because it looked natural. Ma's skin was always the color of milk. She consistently protected herself from the damaging effects of the sun. Now, even women were commenting on how terrific she looked. My mother's head was a study in geriatric comeliness but her body was in a dilapidated state.

Mom was in agony and couldn't walk without dad's assistance. She detested doctors but finally relented and was examined by an orthopedic surgeon. Ma was operated on in luxurious Greenwich Hospital. I'd never seen a medical building that had a grand piano and a male singer dressed in a tuxedo in its lobby which was really an enormous courtyard. His tunes floated to the patients' rooms. Within days of her excruciating procedure, my persuasive mother convinced my gullible father that this medical haven was intolerable. Furthermore, he simply had to "kidnap" her because the doctors did not believe she was strong or well enough to leave. Dad diligently followed orders and brought mom's lapis lazuli and primrose colored caftan, earrings, rings, metallic slippers, and creamy pink lipstick to the hospital. My father somehow got hold of a wheelchair and disengaged the intravenous tubes from my mother's hands and arms. With shunts in her extremities, dad cheerfully rolled my smiling mom to their Lincoln Continental, packed her in, and drove off without signing any release papers.

The staff discovered ma's absence and became hysterical. They believed my mother had been abducted because she was unable to exit the hospital independently. The doctors called the Connecticut State Troopers to investigate her whereabouts. My parents telephoned me in New York City to relay they were on the lam and that they would disown me if I told the cops where they were. Luckily, my folks weren't professional criminals because they couldn't see passed their noses. The first place the police looked for mom was at her residence. They promptly returned a malcontented Claudine to the hospital. I felt like I needed a room too only I required one with rubber walls. From that moment on, I nicknamed dad: Dr. Claude von Bulow.

# Chapter 10

## "My bottom lip is in a pile of manure."

On innumerable occasions new acquaintances and old friends have offered their condolences regarding the fact that I am an only child. Evidently, siblings can help absorb, counteract, redirect, or demystify the bizarre behavior of parents. I've found that loved ones, other than family members and even strangers, can provide the same service. People are also dismayed when they discover that I don't have forty-three cousins and are downright concerned that I haven't reproduced. I cheerfully explain, "I can't miss something I've never had." One Spanish lady remarked, "Oh, my poor woman, who will take care of you when you're old?" Quite frankly, I am elated I don't have to deal with the emotional crap and petty jealousies that darn near everyone on the planet grapples with every day.

I guess those are some of the reasons I never questioned why dad rarely spoke of his relatives. It was as if he had hatched out of a solitary egg in the desert. My father shared only a handful of stories about his youth. I heard about adolescent high jinks such as when he and a chum sat in the backseat of his father's chauffeur driven sedan with a loaded rifle. They took turns shooting holes through its roof. It was a miracle that the boys weren't blinded, deafened, or killed. Grandpa Herbert never punished them for this dangerous escapade. He simply had the car repaired. That incident was a perfect example of how little he cared about his son's welfare and dad's frequent reckless disregard for parental authority.

Milton, my maternal grandfather, never uttered a word about his family in Ireland. Theresa, his wife, showed me one photograph of my German great grandmother. She looked like a portly vicious gun moll that beat puppies for a hobby. I thanked God that her weighty nasty bones were deep in the ground near Heidelberg. Grandma told me a few ghastly stories about how her younger sister died of consumption after not toweling off after a swim. Momps also introduced me to her single brother, skinny Uncle Willy. He smoked himself to death in no time at all. At a young age I accepted the reality that the vast majority of my kin were either six feet under, totally nuts, not worth pursuing, or not interested in my existence. It never bothered me in the least. I actually cherish the peace and quiet of it all. Who the hell cares if I die alone? We all do even if we take our last breath at the Macy's Thanksgiving Day Parade.

My delicate and charismatic great grandmother in Germany.

Dad mentioned that his family spent many a summer at the historic landmark resort, Mohonk Mountain House, which is an enchanting Victorian castle that was turned into a 265-room hotel. This spectacular vacation spot in New Paltz, New York was built in 1869 on Lake Mohonk and is surrounded by 2,200 acres of pristine wilderness. I assumed that Herbert's motive behind these extended extravagant holidays was not driven by a desire to bond with his wife and children but to hunt for potential victims of his Ponzi schemes. Nonetheless, Mohonk is where my father developed a love of horses. Today, experienced guides lead trail rides on scenic carriage roads. Decades ago my father and his brother, Ted, were given powerful horses to ride without a chaperone. Claude and Ted were like mixing gunpowder and dynamite. God knows how they lived to reach adulthood.

My father revisited how Ted almost lost the vision in one eye when his horse reared. Ted's face slammed into the pointy bristles of a cropped mane. To top it off, dad and his brother came close to losing their lives when their horses almost backed off a cliff because of an ornery snake. Of course, these misadventures at Mohonk only fueled my father's passion for riding which in turn sparked my interest many years later.

My parents and I religiously watched the Kentucky Derby and attended the races at a local track. St. Joseph's Elementary School bused female students to a barn where we rode on Wednesday afternoons. The boys went bowling. Evidently, God forbade both genders to simultaneously experience extra-curricular activities. Naturally, my father was pleased when I came home smelling like a jockey. Mom was petrified that I would be paralyzed by a bone crushing fall even though we never even cantered. One afternoon, I took a harmless spill. Mother raced into the arena to rescue me. Her hysterics caused my horse to step on her toes. Luckily, her foot wasn't bruised as her high heel sunk into a mound of straw, mud, and manure. My lessons were discontinued after that scene.

I didn't ride again until I began teaching elementary school. An amiable family at school invited me to join them on their annual trip to England. We flew into Manchester Airport and drove to their vacation home on The North York Moors. I rode the same striking black horse each time we ventured across the magnificent countryside. One splendid morning, two helicopters suddenly appeared out of nowhere and hovered above us. My terrified horse reared and spun until the choppers vanished. I was exhilarated that I hadn't been killed and drank enough whiskey at a nearby pub to calm any fears that might develop on the way back to the barn. The bartender told us that on occasion Prince Charles' pilots veered off course during trainings. After my third shot of booze, I made a pact with myself that I would learn to ride well upon my return to Manhattan.

I began taking lessons at Claremont Riding Academy on the Upper West Side. The oldest stable in the city also provided recreational riding opportunities in nearby Central Park. I became addicted to Claremont for close to ten years. I also visited stables all over New York and New Jersey and partook in various dressage and jumping lessons, paces, and trail rides up to five times a week. I became so devoted to horses that my vacations became equestrian adventures. I wouldn't travel anywhere unless I spent most of my time on horseback. I travelled to England once again and rode on trips to Scotland, Ireland, Switzerland, and the Dominican Republic. When I returned, dad couldn't wait to hear about my rides through ancient forests, along secluded beaches, up and down treacherous mountains, and on scenic country roads. Mom thanked Jesus I was home safely and poured herself another cocktail.

Unfortunately, it's just a matter of time before any rider sustains some form of injury. One night at Claremont, an Appaloosa mare darn near killed me. She decided to put a lip lock on my left forearm as she passed on the outside of the ring. Scarlet threw me to the ground and kept her teeth clenched on my limb as I sat there with my stunned horse's reins in my other hand. No skin was broken but my hand looked like a baseball mitt for a few weeks.

Another time my foot slipped out of its stirrup after making a jump. I fractured some ribs. That was bloody awful because I couldn't do anything for months without wincing in pain. Every exertion from blowing my nose to putting a stick shift in reverse was agonizing. I was also thrown into walls of arenas and blasted through the atmosphere only to land on my derrière on frozen rock hard soil. I couldn't sit down for weeks after those falls.

The worst accident I had occurred when a white mare named Sugar went lame at a canter. It happened at 10:00 at night in a barn in Riverdale, New York, when I was alone with my instructor. I can recall Sugar stumbling. I then assumed a flying position and landed on the right side of my face. My visor stopped the impact to some degree but the back of the helmet struck me in the nape of my neck. I saw a flash of white light and thought for a split second that I had severed my spine. When I was able to stand, I realized that an impression of my facial area was left in the soft dirt. My lower lip was severely injured. I never went to the hospital because I was afraid of what the doctors might do to me.

As luck would have it, the twin brothers of an Indian friend were staying at my apartment in Manhattan. When I got home, their jaws dropped. I drew a warm bath and soaked my bruised body and face until my lip was cleansed. The worried siblings took turns all night long bringing bags of frozen peas to place upon my damaged visage.

By the next morning, I looked like a monster. I missed two weeks of school because I would have scared my students. The inside of my mouth was black. My lip was indescribably grotesque. One side of my face was the color of ebony. I looked like a female version of Quasimodo. My smile was a little crooked for about five years and my lip, though tender, healed with only a few hairline scars which could be covered with lipstick. All telltale signs of my equestrian calamity eventually disappeared. Ripley's Believe It or Not, my love of horses and travelling remained intact after that mishap. After all, life is for living and my hobby took my mind off Claude and Claudine.

## "The ambience is charming except for the smoke."

I began branching out and toured more exotic countries. I figured that Paris and London would always be open to visitors. The French and British would never be able to close their borders to Americans. Maybe they'd like to but they couldn't for economic reasons alone.

I'd leave New York City the day after summer vacation commenced and return the day before teachers had to report for duty in the fall. When I travelled during winter and spring breaks, an inexpensive and reliable car service picked me up to go to the airport directly after dismissal in order to avoid rush hour traffic. This plan worked well because I didn't want to miss a minute of an adventure. These intervals from work lasted a minimum of two weeks at our New York City private school.

I developed two rules for myself when I packed. 1) I was allowed to bring only one mother of a suitcase which I had to be able to maneuver independently. 2) NO CAMERAS! My second dictum flabbergasted people almost as much as the fact that I didn't have a cell phone. Friends actually purchased disposable cameras for me to take on trips. I carefully nestled them between towels in the linen closet before my departure.

Postcards are much better than photographs in my opinion. They are sturdier than snapshots. Plus, you don't have to view strangers you don't give a damn about who are standing in front of a favored sacred site or waste precious time focusing when you could be exploring. Fellow sightseers were often stunned into a state of disbelief when I appeared without a camera. I've received heaps of photos from sympathetic tourists who felt my memory bank was a poor substitution for a Kodak Moment captured on film. I'm grateful for their generosity.

I've been in Brazil on the Amazon River in a dugout canoe in a state of awe only to be stupefied by a holidaymaker who struggled to balance himself because he was tenderly carrying an infant. The babe in arms turned out to be a camera lens dressed in swaddling clothes. Heck, he could have been a giant hors d'oeuvre for a school of piranhas if he fell into those murky waters. I've observed adults lose their senses in Ecuador's Galapagos Islands because they dropped their enormously expensive cameras in the water as they ran for their lives when they got too close to seemingly dormant sea lion bulls.

It doesn't matter if my audience is a close buddy, a total stranger, a circle of cocktail companions, or a group of third graders. I relish sharing anecdotes from distant lands. My students especially enjoy the tale of how I almost perished on the back of an elephant in the jungles of Nepal. The pachyderm took flight because of the sudden appearance of an immature rhinoceros. The terrified giant deduced that the diminutive rhino's mother wasn't far behind. Another favorite is when I rode a pitch black horse through a crack in a mountain. The narrow slit was created by an earthquake and is the spectacular entrance to the lost city of Petra in Jordan.

The little ones chortle as they imagine their teacher hiking in the thin air of Peru to visit a school positioned amongst the clouds. Their mouths are agape as they picture me flat on my back from exhaustion only to be brought back to life by a young boy's offering of a purple potato. The child was endearing but I wished he'd been a paramedic.

Adults prefer the story of how I flew to Cuzco, Peru via Miami dressed in a long black evening dress and stilettos. My baggage was lost en route. I had to purchase an incredibly unflattering hiking outfit to attain my goal of visiting the ancient Incan city of Machu Picchu in the Andes.

Everyone likes to hear about the phenomenal discovery of the life size army of The Terra Cotta Warriors and Horses in Xian, a remote area in northern China. My guide informed me that in 1974, a number of peasants uncovered some pottery while digging for a well. To date 7,000 clay soldiers and horses arranged in battle formation, wooden and bronze chariots, and weapons have been unearthed. Almost all of them have been restored to their former grandeur. Each soldier is an exact replica of its original live model. No two troops are alike. This national landmark is a sight not to be missed. No camera can do it justice.

One of my most treasured yarns concerns my journey from Bombay to New Delhi, India. There's nothing like celebrating New Year's Eve in a maharaja's residence with armed soldiers guarding your door. Yet, that incredible night didn't compare to my visits to the Taj Mahal on the banks of the Yamuna River. Shah Jahan grieved so deeply for the loss of his beloved wife, Mumtaz Mahal, that he created the ultimate symbol of love in Agra. It's truly extraordinary to visit the tomb at various times during the day to observe how different light affects its color. I still find it hard to believe how the sons of Shah Jahan imprisoned their father in a nearby building because he wanted to build an exact replica of the white marble mausoleum in black for himself. That would have been an enormous expense and the kids just didn't go for the idea.

I stayed in a quaint hotel within a few minutes' drive of the memorial. The smog in India is so bad during the winter that I felt as if I had swallowed knife tips on a daily basis. Therefore, I wasn't too surprised to find that my temporary residence hinted of the smell of burning particles. I became concerned as the air became visible in my room. I casually headed to the front desk not wanting to alarm or offend anyone in my host country. When the manager appeared, I politely stated my growing apprehension, "Sir, the ambience of your hotel is charming except for the smoke." He replied in a gracious tone, "Madame, it is simply the pollution." I ingested my umpteenth cherry Halls Mentho Lyptus cough drop and headed off to pay my respects to Mumtaz and her adoring husband. The doomed couple reminded me of Claude and Claudine in a melancholy way. My mother surely would have appreciated a pink Taj Kennedy erected in her honor.

## "The stick shift isn't where it's supposed to be."

It's funny what sticks in your head when you're travelling. I found no truer advice than the warning, "Do NOT enter a kitchen on a tour boat for day trips when sightseeing in China." You'll die of starvation if you do. Let's just say I never imagined so many uses for a shower. After I peeked, I only drank bottled beer and ate rice that afternoon.

Lazy Susans are utilized even in the most stylish restaurants in the Orient. I was mystified by an ever present wooden bowl on a revolving tray which contained marble sized balls of what appeared to be white Wonder Bread. I was advised to swallow a few if I choked on the bones of the fish entrées. Evidently, deboning is not a refined culinary art in much of the East. The doughy pellets force pesky spiny obstacles down one's trachea. Voilà! You're alive when dessert arrives.

I specifically trekked to China to sail upon the mighty Yangtze River before the majestic gorges were flooded. It was amazing to observe a single fisherman on a small raft depend wholeheartedly on the expertise of a trained cormorant for his income. These black diving birds possess a long neck that expands to swallow fish. However, the feathered bread winners have a ring placed around their throats when they work so they cannot swallow their catch. They dutifully place their game at the feet of their owners. Periodically, the skillful birds are allowed to ingest a live meal as a treat. Who knew there were winged laborers that work long, hard hours in China?

Cotton balls fascinated me in the majestic Himalayas and in the deepest rain forests of Brazil. At times, it is necessary for thrill-seeking travelers to fly in military planes that are not equipped with the luxury of pressurized cabins. Such aircraft are fitted with rustic seats which line the interior of the fuselage. Heavy cargo, crates of food, and luggage are stored in the tail of the plane and are clearly visible to all passengers. Tiny windows are so far above eye level that they provide minimal light. The seat belts look like they were recruited from a garbage bin after needy soldiers were provided with something more efficient to hold up their pants.

It is standard procedure on such planes for a wicker basket filled with dingy cotton balls of questionable origin to be circulated amongst an assorted cast of characters. At first, I couldn't figure out what the white fluffy orbs were used for so their tattered straw container left my hands quicker than a deployed hand grenade. I also didn't see the necessity of tightening my security harness until my eyes bulged out of their sockets; silly me.

I discovered that a gradual take off is not generally practiced in such airborne vehicles. On one occasion in the heart of South America, I felt as if I unwittingly participated in a rocket launch. I was positive that my eardrums were shattered when we shot into the atmosphere. My body was catapulted through the main aisle of the aircraft and landed in a pile of army supplies. I was dazed but managed a girlish smile as either horrified or apathetic faces glanced at my crumpled figure. I didn't dare move until I was sure that the plane had leveled off. When I returned to my empty seat, I strapped myself in like a deceased buck on top of a Land Rover and stuffed enough cotton in each ear to fill a teddy bear. This is a cautionary tale. Tighten your seat belt for God's sake and if someone hands you cotton on an airplane, be damn sure to use it.

My father adored hearing every detail of my adventures. I simply sent picturesque postcards to my mother affirming the excellent state of my health and that I loved her more than anything else on the planet. Upon my return, dad sat quietly and listened to my whispered tales so mom couldn't hear a word. His lips parted slightly like a child's when I described my adventures in the air in Kenya.

The author hopping from one hemisphere to another in Kenya.

Quite a few of my days in East Africa began long before the sun rose. My extravagant tent was better equipped than most homes. It was raised about two feet above the ground and had polished slate floors, roomy closets, modern plumbing, and electrical conveniences. Each morning, hot chocolate was delivered to my abode before I began my explorations. However, there were a few unique requirements regarding the upkeep of my well-being. I had to zip up my home each night and tie a slew of double knotted bows to ensure that I wasn't mauled by curious and hungry baboons. After dinner, I had to walk briskly to my sleeping area with a flashlight. I was warned to listen for any sounds behind me because there was a chance that I'd be attacked and eaten by wild cats. No worries; I adored every minute of my time in the jungle.

One morning a few hours before dawn, I arose to prepare for a long-awaited ride in a thermal airship. My party drove to an open plain where our colorful and empty hot air balloon lay stretched out upon the ground. To my delight, I learned that I was to ride in one of the world's largest airships. Two gondolas, each holding six people, would fly through the early morning currents. After a noisy period of filling the balloon, our baker's dozen which included the pilot piled in for a jaunt of a lifetime.

We soared over exquisite landscape and a vast assortment of wild animals in their glorious homeland. The pilot was a bit foolhardy. At times it seemed as if our lives were of secondary importance. He would unexpectedly make the airship plunge through the air until the bottoms of our wicker baskets were inches above a river filled with bathing hippopotami. Their broad and cavernous mouths angrily snapped at us. Good God, it was exciting.

This spectacular ride lasted a couple of hours. Just before landing on a plain in the middle of nowhere, we were instructed to perch on a narrow ledge just above the floor of our baskets and to hold on tightly. We slammed into the Earth. The gondolas suddenly flipped onto their sides and dragged us along the ground on our backs at a forceful speed. When the balloon finally came to a halt, we were grabbed under our armpits, hauled out, and unceremoniously placed in a standing position by extremely tall thin guards who were equipped with rifles and spears. Lo and behold, it was time for our first meal of the day.

My stunned fellow passengers and I were led to a humongous dining table smack dab in the middle of Kenya's Masai Mara National Park. We drank champagne and consumed one of the most delicious breakfasts I've ever had the pleasure of eating. Perhaps it seemed so tasty because of the danger involved. Our armed escorts surrounded us and keenly observed our surroundings so we wouldn't become snacks for lions. Dad was green with envy and mom darn near fainted when I related these events at one of their holiday get-togethers.

Some stories I kept to myself or shared with my closest comrades. My parents never heard much about my travels in Italy except for the fantastic food and incredible sightseeing. I spent two fabulous summers there. The only regret I had was leaving before I could experience a Tuscan autumn. I stayed with close friends in Rome, Florence, Sardinia, and in a magnificent area known as Umbria.

I had the honor of deciding what we'd explore on many of our delightful outings. We thought it would be a terrific idea to choose themes. I was mad about the Etruscan civilization. Therefore, we tracked down the location of underground *hypogeum* or beautifully painted multiple tomb chambers, climbed down into them, and gaped at the magnificence of ancient times. On that particular day, my limited Italian vocabulary increased by two very important words, *"Attenzione, vipere!"* Even I didn't require a translator for such a catchy phrase, "Caution, snakes!"

Another topic that I wanted to pursue was anything to do with volcanoes. We commenced our study by packing a lip-smacking picnic and quite a few bottles of vino. Five of us drove to an extraordinary lake which is actually a crater filled with invigorating cold water in Subiaco. This attractive town holds the distinct honor of being the birthplace of Lucrezia Borgia and Gina Lollobrigida. We rented four *pedalos* which are small pleasure boats that are powered by human legs. Each vehicle had a flat area behind its two seats which was as big as a table for four people. We tied our vessels together so the sterns touched one another. It was easy to walk back and forth amongst our crafts. We ate, drank, smoked, sunbathed, swam, and enjoyed an exceptionally refreshing afternoon.

Staving off the heat in the evenings was a priority because there was no air conditioning in our flat in Rome. After a scrumptious meal at one of the many excellent *trattorias* in the neighborhood, we'd sit and laugh in a blissful state until the wee hours of the morning. The Italians were amazed by my remedy to keep us cool. Night after night, I placed my hosts' and their guests' feet and forearms in pots and pans filled to the brim with cold water and a few ice cubes. Sighs of delight and relief lingered in the air as bottles of wine were passed. After my departure to the United States, my low cost method of chilling heated bodies continued into the fall.

I was the driver whenever we travelled in Italy. Hours were spent speeding along the *Autostrada* which makes Interstate 95 look like a kiddy ride at Disney World. The legal speed limit is approximately 80 mph for cars. There were always people who found the pace too slow. When I made the error of not getting out of their way fast enough, they repeatedly flashed their headlights and rode my back fender until they were practically in the trunk.

One afternoon as we were returning to Rome after sightseeing, our Fiat's stick shift disengaged itself. I turned to my friends, waved the broken car part in the air, and calmly announced, "The stick shift isn't where it's supposed to be. We're going to die." Screams and nervous laughter engulfed us as I held the steering wheel with one hand and frantically screwed the gearshift back into place with the other hand. Of course, we repeatedly toasted our survival that night. We were thankful that we didn't make the evening news as the latest fiery heap of metal on that notorious freeway.

Alas, my travelling days on Alitalia Airline came to a standstill when my folks decided to move down south. I rarely considered flying from The Big Apple to The Sunshine State as a sought after pleasure trip. My visits to Claude and Claudine became a routine that transformed into an obligation which I felt was my karmic duty to fulfill. It turns out that every one of my journeys whether they were to Seville, Spain, or Atlantis, Florida was an intricate part of my destiny. Oddly enough, I didn't really mature into a full-fledged adult until I experienced life in plain old Palm Beach County, USA.

# Chapter 11

## "I'd like you to meet Ganesh and Shiva."

My parents rented a bedroom and a bathroom in a divorcee's home in Lake Worth, Florida after residing in an assortment of motels. Ma and dad had the place to themselves for most of the day because their middle-aged landlord, Sue, worked as an accountant. She owned a large house which reflected her Hindu heritage. The home's modern décor was accented with a collection of ceramic replicas of ancient gods and goddesses and a dog-less dog run.

Not only had my parents left me high and dry in New York City, they left the fourth member of our little family with me. Muffy III was an adorable, cream-colored, spoiled, highly intelligent, and deeply sensitive toy poodle. The needy pooch swiftly turned into a manic depressive without her beloved Claude and Claudine present to coddle her at every given moment. Muffy had been hugged, cooed at, and continually fed freshly baked warm chicken and cookies from the moment she entered their Greenwich, Connecticut apartment. To my disbelief, she was unexpectedly dumped at my Upper West Side apartment and forced to live with me, a Montessori teacher, who worked long hours and spent the rest of the time horseback riding, partying, or sleeping.

Muff couldn't bare the mongrel ruffians in Central Park. I was miserable and felt guilty leaving her alone for so many hours. I was also going broke speeding uptown in a cab every chance I got to take her out to pee. I reluctantly hired Felix, a bohemian dog walker. I came home unexpectedly one afternoon and spotted a delicate and doleful Muffster walking with five massive canines. She barely made it back to the apartment alive.

I promptly fired Felix and hired his girlfriend. My newly acquired poodle despised Lisa from the get-go. However, she specialized in taking care of small dogs and there was no one else in my neighborhood who shared her occupation. These two entrepreneurs made a bloody fortune off our community of thoroughly desperate dog owners. After hours of pricey group therapy on my living room floor, Muff eventually allowed Lisa to care for her. Even with Lisa's help, I knew I had to deliver my parents' precious pet to Florida in the very near future.

I also wanted to get my folks settled in a home of their own. Months had passed. Sue was content with the extra cash and their distinctive company. I just couldn't understand why the process of finding a respectable residence was taking so long. After all, they had the cash from the sale of the apartment in Connecticut. I decided it was time to call Jet Blue and get Muffy the heck out of The Big Apple and head to The Big Orange.

I departed from frigid New York City with my parents' temporary address in one hand and a hysterical poodle in the other. Jet Blue kindly offered to provide a petite kennel crate. Little did I know that a minute carrier, just large enough for a small rabbit, was mistakenly reserved for Muffy. I promptly folded her and spent the entire flight in a painful yoga position attempting to comfort the pitiful poodle as she was now stuffed under the seat in front of me.

The Muffster and I finally arrived at the Floridian version of the Taj Mahal. Tears of relief initially blurred my clear vision of where my folks were staying. I gave them a quick introduction to the basic Hindi deities and promptly began the quest for the home I eventually would call my own.

## "We live in The Lost City of Atlantis."

I had a week off from school for spring break. Muffy and I arrived on Sue's doorstep on a bright Sunday morning. Dad looked reasonably well but mom was weaker than ever. Her radiant and loving smile was the same but she couldn't remain standing for more than a few moments. Time was of the essence. My parents had to live in a stable and safe environment. I didn't know Florida from a hole-in-the-wall. In fact, I thought Florida was a hole-in-the-wall.

Sue, dad, and I examined <u>The Palm Beach Post's</u> real estate section. We found a few places that seemed viable. As my parents and I set off for a day of house hunting, Sue handed me a tiny newspaper clipping about a villa for sale in the city of Atlantis which is located within the city of Lake Worth. I chuckled and thought, "How appropriate for my parents to live in The Lost City of Atlantis which sunk into the Atlantic Ocean and was never found."

Every prospective home we visited had something wrong with it. Muffy would be a mouthwatering tidbit if we had a canal full of alligators in the backyard. Some houses were lovely but literally in the middle of nowhere. Our last stop on the way back to Sue's was Atlantis. She mentioned that the city was a former Brahman cattle ranch so we didn't expect much more than a few cow patties. We were pleasantly surprised to find that Atlantis is one of the most picturesque, pristine, and safe country club communities in the United States. There's even a private airport nearby. Best of all, JFK Medical Center is located on Atlantis' property. Every type of doctor and medical equipment anyone could ever need plus a slew of ambulances are just a stone's throw away. A potpourri of ethnic restaurants, hairdressers, a fitness center, Home Depot, movie theaters, a post office, a library, a variety of schools, Publix grocery stores, and numerous gas stations are less than five minutes from The Lost City. The majestic Atlantic Ocean and major shopping malls are also only ten minutes away. Atlantis offers mansions, smaller homes, townhouses, a variety of apartments, and villas to suit almost any taste and budget. The moment we walked into one of the older villas, I knew it was the place for us. I convinced dad to negotiate on the spot. Sue had a trustworthy lawyer who helped him close the deal. Claude, Claudine, and Muffy III moved into their new dwelling on May 1, 2001.

Unbeknownst to me, dad had the contents of their Greenwich, Connecticut apartment in storage. Bravo, daddio! All he had to do was make a phone call and everything would be delivered to the house in Florida in a few weeks. I breathed a sigh of relief as I believed a new and more carefree cycle was beginning for my parents. They seemed happy as larks whenever I spoke to them on the phone. Sue and a few of her friends helped bring their belongings to Atlantis. The Connecticut movers did their job. I was freed from worrying about Claude and Claudine for fourteen days.

Sue called me late one night in Manhattan and swore me to secrecy. She promised my folks she would not inform me that mom was recuperating from a near fatal fall. I was dumbfounded as Sue explained that my mother was literally navy blue on the entire left side of her body due to severe injuries. I almost didn't believe the trustworthy accountant because I religiously called my parents four or five times a week to check on them.

Sue told me she stopped by as a surprise with a house warming gift and was appalled by what she saw. My father had unpacked a few dishes and utensils and that was the extent of it. All of mom and dad's possessions were once again in layers of boxes up to the ceiling. There was a path through the cartons from the front door which forked to the right and led to the kitchen. The countertops were cluttered with boxes and bags of half eaten fast foods. The trail to the left led to my parents' bedroom and bathroom.

That would have been bad enough but Sue continued with her astoundingly ghoulish narrative. Mother had fallen on the unfamiliar tile flooring and smashed her left shoulder to smithereens. She was on the dressing room floor in unbearable pain for two days. Mom refused to allow dad to call an ambulance. My obedient father covered ma with blankets and kept a steady flow of vodka heading her way. On the third day he miraculously decided to call our handyman, Leo, to scrape my delirious mother off the floor. Thank God Leo had enough sense to notify the hospital and not listen to my irrational dad. Atlantis had a new doctor in town. Dr. Claude von Bulow was at it again.

## "I lost fifteen pounds visiting my parents!"

Mercifully, my summer vacation from teaching allowed me to hop on a plane to survey the damage. Passing through the guarded gates of Atlantis in a cab from the airport was like entering an earthly paradise. Crossing the threshold of my parents' front door was similar to getting sucked through a portal which led straight to hell. My mother looked like a smiling, undernourished, female version of <u>The Phantom of the Opera</u> except for the fact she wasn't wearing a mask. Her anemia was so severe that it took ages for hematomas to heal. A surgeon had inserted pins in her shoulder to hold it together. She had her arm in a sling and was in bed with a cocktail in her free hand. Dad was stationed about five feet away in front of the television. He was surrounded by mounds of packs of cigarettes and empty over-the-counter asthma inhalers. Muffy looked like she was left unattended in the Everglades for months.

My new best friends were sanitation workers and anyone who sold cleaning products. I ingested a large plate full of protein and carbohydrates each morning. Little Claudie then worked like a horse until late at night when I possessed just enough strength to fall asleep. My so-called bed was a white fold-out sofa which would have crippled Conan the Barbarian.

Some of the crates I had to empty were extremely heavy. Therefore, I beckoned any man or large woman who walked or drove by to help me avoid permanent spinal damage. I motivated electricians, landscapers, and telephone repair people to leave their posts with mouthwatering trays of icy ginger ale and stacks of crispy graham crackers. They would then move bulky pieces of furniture or hang cumbersome mirrors. In the ungodly Floridian summer sun, offerings of infinite amounts of cold beverages and sugary treats worked wonders.

I assumed my relatives would use actual suitcases to pack their belongings when moving to another state. Wrong again. Try countless flimsy white plastic grocery bags, the back seat of their 1994 Lincoln Continental, and its enormous trunk. More than half a year after their unconventional drive from Connecticut to Florida, I ventured into the posterior abyss of the Lincoln with the mistaken notion I could actually place groceries in that humongous compartment. I was astonished to find innumerable pairs of mismatched stilettos which mom hadn't worn since 1965, more than a dozen formal evening gowns, a box of fossilized chocolates, old Valentine's Day cards signed with heart wrenching proclamations of love from Claude to Claudine, squashed boxes of Kleenex and Wheat Thins, blankets, half used jars of Vaseline, crumpled girlie magazines, and an untold number of empty bottles of club soda, Coca Cola, scotch, vodka, gin, crème de menthe, and tequila. What really boggled my mind was the fact that I already unpacked the same crap from the backseat of the Lincoln weeks ago.

My parents were thrilled to have their "pride and joy" around the house. Their "baby girl" was more like a cursing and depressed Hulk Hogan. After about a month and a half of manual labor, their villa of madness looked like a home. Life in Florida was improving. Ma had healed somewhat and looked like she was severely jaundiced and married to a wife beater. She occasionally consented to eat an egg salad sandwich without the crust if it was cut on a diagonal and measured no more than a square inch. Tom Thumb would have been insulted by such dainty portions. Muffy was groomed and ate regularly. She was glad to have a companion who wasn't in bed all day or covered with cinders. Dad was not allowed to smoke in the house but was happy to leave "his girls" to further destroy his lungs on the patio or in the carport up to thirty times a day. He was well fed and strangely quiet but seemed content having his dwindling family around him.

My parents were more than grateful for my assistance and told me so on an hourly basis. I left in early September feeling secure that my father could hold the fort until my winter vacation from school. I was fifteen pounds lighter, possessed muscles of steel, and couldn't wait to return to my life in New York City.

## "Would you like to sit in the golf cart and have a drink?"

By the time I returned to celebrate the holidays in Atlantis, Claude, Claudine, and Muffy had developed a bizarre nightly ritual. Maybe that's what warm weather does to some individuals. Starting on the day of my arrival, I noticed that all three of them were unconscious by 8 p.m. I quietly kept myself amused by cooking, cleaning, polishing, dusting, scrubbing, sorting, washing, rinsing, drying, flushing, draining, emptying, vacuuming, mopping, folding, unfolding, and perspiring until midnight. Like clockwork the three vampires arose from their shared king size casket. They began to intermittently snack, drink, talk, laugh, cuddle, watch TV, and eventually sit in their prized golf cart which I had surprised them with for their fiftieth anniversary.

Mom and Muffy parked themselves in the front seat of the mini-vehicle. It was a perfect height for them to easily maneuver into and had a nifty cup holder to secure mother's Gibson Martini. The cart was housed in a covered passageway in the carport where their dinosaur of a Lincoln also rested its weary body. Dad often sat in a large white wrought iron chair. Claude and Claudine chatted lightheartedly like teenagers about how much they loved each other, their little dog, their antiquated car, their new home, and most of all, their tireless daughter. This routine continued until approximately four in the morning.

My father slept for about three more hours, dressed, and took Muffy on his rounds. He purchased a few drops of gas, packs of cigarettes, a handful of inhalers to help him breathe, The Wall Street Journal, The New York Post, The New York Times, fashion magazines, and perhaps a cookie or two to munch on and share with the Muffster as they drove home. Next, they made themselves comfortable in bed beside mom and read, watched TV, snoozed, and nibbled all day until cocktail hour. Dad then assisted mom with her dressing and primping. My folks headed out to a local watering hole for a couple of drinks and a bite to eat. Some nights I tagged along to inspect their hangouts and wondered why my mother hadn't succumbed to second hand smoke decades ago. Bartenders and the regulars fell in love with them and looked forward to their entertaining visits. My parents arrived home in time to feed Muffy a warmed chicken breast which was cut into tiny bite size pieces and let her out for a stroll in the backyard. They all hit the sack and drifted into their respective comas until the appointed witching hour. After a couple of weeks, I was used to their strange and predictable drills. In any case, they were happy and safe.

The four of us spent a quiet Christmas together. My father purchased his usual giant Hallmark testimony of holiday love, white silk panties, lacey handkerchiefs, and chocolates for mom. She was delighted. Mom presented dad with a kiss and a hug for Christmas. That was all she had to give and it completely satisfied him.

During my summer of arranging their belongings, I came across a dusty rolled up print of a Sioux warrior ready for battle. Dad purchased this signed piece of graphic art in New Mexico in the early 1980's. It was a portrait of an independent and virile man deep in contemplation as he clutched a lethal feathered spear and sat upon his horse. Both were covered in war paint as dark thunder clouds loomed overhead. I believe my father related to this solemn combatant. Their lives were similarly filled with deadly skirmishes with fate.

Dad cherished this subconscious representation of himself but was never able to display it because it clashed with the décor of their homes. I had it framed and hung so he could gaze at it from bed. On Christmas morning I undraped his long lost soul mate. Like an excited youngster he told mom, "Little Claudie sure knows how to give good gifts!" I also gave him some handmade coupons from me for pedicures because he couldn't reach his feet anymore and a few for back rubs which he cashed in for thirty minutes of relief from muscles that felt as if they had turned to stone.

I gave mom a series of manicures and pedicures and painted her nails with her favorite glimmering white metallic polish. I buffed her stacks of silver tea sets, candelabra, platters, vases, pitchers, ashtrays, jewelry cases, and cutlery, and cleaned her chandeliers and rings until they sparkled. I waited until evening and turned on subtle lighting so the sterling and chandeliers glimmered. Her eyes welled up with tears. Perhaps memories of swinging soirees danced through her mind.

That same summer I discovered two of ma's abandoned and exquisite needlepoint creations of birds which she designed during the years she perched by her dying father's bedside. For Christmas I had one of them made into a heart shaped pillow with pink grosgrain fabric on one side and a regal cardinal, her favorite feathered friend, on the other. I figured mom loved birds because they could fly away at any time. She, on the other hand, was often grounded by misery. I also had a butler pull made from a panel of her embroidered birds flying towards the heavens. It was decorated with intricate brass hardware at the top and on the bottom. Mom always wanted a butler. Now and forever, Claudine had Claude, a faithful round-the-clock helper who worshipped her.

# Chapter 12

**"How about a subscription to <u>Tits and Ass</u>?"**

New Year's Eve was a real eye opener. Mother was dressed in an ethereal, white, formal, pants suit with a V-neck adorned with a wide taffeta collar that framed her face. All night long, strangers stopped by the table to tell mom how lovely she looked. After the last verse of "Auld Lang Syne" was sung and the confetti settled into the carpet, I paid a waiter to carry her to the car. From that moment on, I was haunted by the possibility that one or both of my parents might not be around much longer. The phantom of declining health once again chilled me to the bone.

The dynamic duo rebounded by noon on New Year's Day. The house would have made Mr. Clean beam with satisfaction. The cupboards were filled with every food, drink, and supply imaginable. My family would have been able to survive for quite some time if a nuclear blast occurred. I arranged for neighbors to keep an eye on them. I also hired a cleaning lady to tidy up the place once a week and report to me what she observed. My folks' grins, promises, and false sense of faith in themselves eased my trepidation as I departed for Manhattan.

Six calamity free months passed quickly. My telephone bill was enormous but my mind was relieved with every call. Jet Blue once again delivered me to The Sunshine State. By now, I had a driver/gopher named Joe who helped me through the maze of caring for my parents from afar. I didn't want dad to pick me up at the airport anymore because it seemed too much of a task. Claude and Claudine greeted me with open arms. Muffy almost jumped out of her skin with joy.

I was tickled and amazed as I walked into my parents' villa. They had renovated the den by removing all of the shelves and built-in desk areas. Dad had a Murphy queen size bed installed. It was the best architectural move he ever made. My father had created a bedroom for me. However, there was an incredible amount of furniture in this twelve by thirteen foot chamber. I applied my make-up on a gigantic carved wooden bar with a brass footrest. I placed my jewelry on my deceased grandmother's red chinoiserie styled piano. I rested my books and school work on my grandpa's desk. I positioned my sun hat on a male Grecian bust which stood upon a majestic marble stand and stared at me until I fell asleep. I watched David Letterman or Jay Leno on a battery operated black and white television with a five inch screen that sat upon an antique cabinet. Strangely enough there was seating for five very cramped people but no lamps so you were out of luck after the sun went down. My luggage rested on cushiony, new, white carpet which flowed throughout most of the house.

I was thrilled to see The Three Musketeers again. Throughout the summer, I continued to clean, shop, cook, organize, rearrange, and keep the villa and everyone in it in order. At this point, I was able to swim and relax by the pool for hours at a time. Barnes & Noble became my intellectual and spiritual oasis. I devoured self-help books with the hope they would assist me in making myself stronger and wiser. No literature has been written that could have prepared me for what was to come. It's advantageous that humans don't have access to crystal balls to see their futures. Hara-kiri might well become a fad.

My newest growing concern was the fact dad was less talkative. I concluded that the pressure of taking care of mom was getting to him. He was glued to the television night and day. My mother seemed unnerved by what he was viewing so I decided to watch too.

I damn near died. First, all I heard was wild drumming like the heartbeat of an ape in heat. I thought maybe he was into some sort of tropical dance craze. I then realized he was watching video after video after video. He had a collection large enough for the Library of Congress. Horror Hotel, my father had become obsessed with <u>Girls Gone Wild</u>! My poor, defenseless, crippled, and sickly mother was a trapped audience. In her naiveté, she believed dad was watching national TV stations and the whole country had gone to the dogs.

Dad had ordered one smutty tape right after they moved to Florida but didn't understand that he had been bamboozled into receiving another one every month to the tune of $27 apiece. Of course, each video was automatically charged to his VISA account which he no longer inspected. Wild ads and magazines began arriving at the house. God knows what the mailman thought. I never imagined such devices for so-called sexual pleasure and with so many people involved. As far as I'm concerned, consenting adults can do anything with anyone. I simply didn't care for pictures of such scenes being delivered to the front door into the hands of my father. I couldn't comprehend what had come over formerly docile Claude. The final straw was when I answered the phone and a creepy male voice asked me if I wanted a subscription to <u>Tits and Ass</u>. I almost had a stroke and proceeded to turn his ear blue. He never called back.

The sanitation workers adored me more than ever now. They had been pleased with ginger ale and graham crackers. The guys couldn't believe the jackpot they hit when I handed them boxes of pornography. Our villa was the most popular garbage stop for miles.

# "There's a reason for twenty years of poor decisions."

Praise the Lord, another Christmas arrived and everyone was still alive. As usual, Joe dropped me off at my parents' abode and the merriment began. There were hugs, kisses, squeals, compliments, and tears galore at my family's reunion. Each time we gathered was sweeter than the last because no one knew if there'd be another meeting with all of us present. With a superficial glance around the place, everything appeared to be relatively normal with a few exceptions. The glass covered white wrought iron table which seated six in the Florida Room was covered with stacks of papers about two inches thick. I picked up the phone to call a friend in New York and it was dead. What had happened here? Better yet, what had not happened here?

I started to sort a variety of unpaid bills, unopened bank statements, overdue insurance notices, letters from dad's accountant and stock advisor, and other various pieces of unsettling correspondence. I asked my father questions about the state of his financial affairs and the general upkeep of the house. He was vague and uncharacteristically nervous and defensive. I stared into his big, dark brown eyes which were surrounded by coal black eyelashes. They were so thick and long that mom and I used to tease him, "If we turned you upside down, we could use you as a broom." I was dumbfounded as I realized I didn't recognize the man looking back at me. I let the matter drop and escorted him back to his revered television.

I thought back to dad's father's affliction of compulsive gambling. That connection didn't make sense to me. I remembered that his mother was mentally incapable by the age of forty. Supposedly, she had developed early onset Alzheimer's disease. I began to put two and two together.

Mom was the center of attention during the last decade. Nobody, including myself, really noticed that dad only responded to simple questions. He was unable to carry on a detailed conversation. My father became a master at appearing to take part in a discussion. I took it personally and was hurt that he no longer chatted with me when I called from New York but handed the phone to mom.

I felt that maybe he was miffed at me for not doing more even though I was bending over backwards to assist them. I recalled all the poor financial and medical decisions he'd made over the last twenty plus years. I pictured him ages ago at our home in New York at 4 a.m. in the kitchen, smoking cartons of Tareytons, eating Wheat Thins, and staring blankly at the television screen. I recollected the aberrant behavior with the sex videos. I presumed that he liked wearing the same old clothes all the time because they were comfortable. A few weeks earlier, mom mentioned in one of her calls that dad went to pick up some of her medicine and didn't return for over three hours. It was only a five minute ride to the store. She said that he had gotten lost. I realized my father couldn't remember how to get home.

I looked around the villa and noticed inhalers scattered everywhere. I wondered if his intense smoking and diminished lung capacity due to severe emphysema were cutting off oxygen to his brain. I kept running possibilities through my head like numbers being fed into a calculator. I recognized the heartbreaking truth of the matter in the middle of the night when I could not sleep. My dear father, who had been afflicted with so many trials and tribulations throughout his entire life, had been stricken with dementia for God knows how long. The puzzle pieces fit together and depicted a vision of the future which made me close my eyes and shiver.

## "Don't bother picking me up."

There was another upsetting addition to the mix at the villa this Christmas. Mom began falling down more often. It was a surreal déjà vu in a medical sense. I recalled how dad experienced many hurtful tumbles before his back operation. Now, I saw for myself how ma bounced from room to room. Thank baby Jesus most of the villa was covered with white carpet with padding underneath to cushion her unexpected descents.

It appeared that my parents had taken up wrestling as a hobby. My heart was in my mouth as I observed my mother gracefully slide to the floor and insist that she was quite comfortable residing there in a ladylike lump. Ma would then request a cocktail, sip contentedly, and chat with dad who rested in a nearby chair. Eventually the tug of war, hugging, and laughing began as Claude valiantly attempted to maintain Claudine in a semi-vertical position. Sometimes when she hit the bricks outside but did not injure herself, my father and I simply gave up and called the fire department. Unfailingly, benevolent giants lifted her without breaking a sweat and delivered mom to her boudoir. Paramedics used a plank of wood to scoop her up if she was in a tight position. Everyone was always in the best of spirits and chuckling all the while because ma was still bewitching even in her unenviable condition.

I continued to research the effects of dementia. It was evident the disorder was taking an increasingly devastating hold upon dad. I read that such cognitive deterioration progressed at a faster rate when the victim was under stress, never mind the daily strain of caring for my mother. In addition, the intellectual ability to make reasonable decisions decreased. This was definitely the case with my father's driving. He had already side swiped two cars on separate occasions and called me in New York to pay off the owners of the damaged vehicles. Dad was very lucky that those accidents only cost a few thousand dollars and not the remaining shreds of shirt off his back.

I eventually hid the car keys. Even worse, I sometimes lied and told dad that he must have the keys because I didn't know where they were. My father also used the cigarette lighter in the Lincoln in the middle of the night. I unhappily realized this strange habit caused the battery to die as I attempted to run morning errands. This maddening surprise occurred on a regular basis. Our benevolent mechanics felt so sorry for me that they recharged the car's battery for free. It wasn't because of my charms or good looks. I resembled road kill when I was in Florida. My hair was doused with chlorine and looked like hay from swimming each day. I wore dresses from Publix grocery store, no make-up, and rubber flip-flops. Nonetheless, I still managed to look better than half the population.

This trip to Florida proved to me that ten thousand phone calls, reports from friendly neighborhood spies, plus visits during Christmas and summer vacations were no longer sufficient to ensure my parents' well-being. I knew it was going to be necessary to visit Atlantis on spring breaks and, on occasion, three-day weekends. My winter hiatus turned into a struggle to convince my folks that it would be easier for me to handle their finances.

I found that my elderly parents didn't trust their own "child" to pay their bills. At first, Claude and Claudine adamantly rejected the esoteric concept of monthly automatic withdrawals from their bank account. With their permission, I gradually compiled numerous documents and account statements before I flew back to New York. Within a few months of my return to Manhattan, I was able to manage all of their medical, financial, legal, and mechanical needs over the phone or by mail. That meant I was required to haul around a hideous, sage green, plastic, expandable, ten pound file everywhere I went. This mobile library accompanied me in my car, at school, and on planes. I never knew when an emergency might arise and I'd need mom and dad's social security numbers, birth dates, or blood types. When a situation arose, I found it much less confounding to have all of the information I needed at my fingertips.

My bulky dossier became a priceless Bible to me and contained the names, telephone numbers, and addresses of anyone who could help my mother and father. There was a section for the Atlantis police and fire departments, Atlantis garbage and recycling collection, Atlantis Utilities, Florida Power & Light, AT & T, Comcast Cable TV, Blue Cross/Blue Shield, doctors, their dentist, a pharmacist, the JFK Medical Center emergency room, dad's accountant and lawyer, a stock broker, our mechanics, a plumber, an electrician, a handyman, the gardener, all of our neighbors, the villa association president, an air conditioner and appliance repair person, exterminators, a mobile dog grooming company, and various cleaning services. I decided that it was better to build a few muscles lugging around my plastic parental profile than incinerate my brain cells when a problem arose.

## "They didn't shift gears for more than fifty years!"

Months elapsed. Dad continued to talk less and less but still managed to purchase food and make meals. He also bought other goodies. My folks somehow managed to forge an illegal affiliation with a physician in the nearby town of Lantana. I nicknamed him Dr. Feelgood. Any type of pill my parents thought they might need was provided by this quack. He had never even met my mother. Yet, he prescribed a vast array of medications: diuretics, sleeping pills, antibiotics, and tranquilizers. You name it; no problem. Sadly and thankfully, dad couldn't remember how to get to this con artist's home any more. That's how I stumbled upon and promptly terminated the influx of drugs into our villa.

The maid I hired to clean my parents' residence informed me that she quit because it was "too dangerous a place to work." She didn't "want to get blamed for my mother and father's sicknesses" or "sued if they fell." Swell news. I began to feel like I was juggling expensive China on a high wire without a net. Other than Gert, our dear but fragile neighbor, there was no one else to help me in sunny Florida. I never had the opportunity to know my paternal grandparents, aunts, uncles, or cousins. My mother and father decided decades ago that mental illness, criminal activity, and personality conflicts were sufficient grounds to make it impossible for me to see any relatives other than Mr. and Mrs. Reliable, Pops and Momps. Therefore, I groped in the dark with the question that plagued me day and night, "What in the world am I going to do for my parents?" When I was a teenager, I vowed to mom that I would always take care of her and dad which meant I would never put either of them in a home. Fortunately, divine guidance is often granted when an intention is focused on helping others. Who knew that a summer evening stroll with Muffy in Atlantis would prolong my parents' lives and safeguard my sanity?

Our brilliant, hard-working, and duty-bound neighbor who is a magistrate lived with her mom and learned many of life's lessons taking care of her fatally ill father. Diane advised me to contact Hospice of Palm Beach County as her chihuahua and my poodle danced around one another. I was puzzled because I was under the impression that Hospice only treated dying people. In my humble opinion, my parents weren't in that category quite yet.

Diane explained that Hospice cares for sickly family members in countless ways. This organization of saints provides high quality medical care, doctors, nurses, aides, therapists, masseuses, clerics, musicians, and barbers at no charge. Hospice also makes arrangements for the delivery of medicines, hospital furniture, and therapeutic equipment to your address. Psychological, religious, and financial counseling are also available for free. Social workers and trained volunteers shop, run errands, read to, and visit with patients. A Hospice related company called Helping Hands sends staff to your home so primary caretakers can have some priceless private time for themselves. It was as if I had been subjected to a famine and Diane led me to a banquet.

Within a few days, I made the necessary calls and vaguely explained my intentions to my folks. When the team arrived to make their initial evaluations, Claude and Claudine met them with a ten foot thick wall of hostile resistance. I conferred with the Hospice associates and was faced with the harsh reality that not only was my mother speedily accepted into the program but my father needed immediate medical attention too. I was also informed that it would be in my mom and dad's best interest if I moved to Florida, pronto. My jaw hit the tiles. I wanted to do all I could for them but leaving New York City and quitting my job wasn't a viable option. How could I leave my friends, school, and the culture and vibrancy of Manhattan? Florida was the epitome of a "no man, woman, or child's land" to me. I pictured scads of surfers and drifters unconscious on the beaches from overdosing on margaritas and shirtless lifeguards posing as elected government officials. Yes, there were polo matches in Wellington in season and a massage at the Four Seasons Resort once every light year but who could be trusted to trim my hair?

Mom was diagnosed with the most peculiar ailment I ever heard of: Failure to Thrive. This condition actually killed people! I imagined how cancer cells reproduced wildly and corroded vital organs or how a violent car crash took lives instantaneously. How in God's name could moving from a house to an apartment to a modest villa develop into a death sentence for my mother?

I recognized that the standard problem with many people of my parents' generation was that they never altered their belief systems to accommodate the changes taking place around them. Claude and Claudine couldn't get to a voting machine if their lives depended on it but steadfastly declared they would cast their ballots for any Republican until the day they died. It didn't faze them that George Walker Bush flushed our nation down the proverbial loo. I grinned as I recollected when I initially registered as a Socialist during my tormented teens. I believed that neither the Democrats nor the Republicans could save our country. I almost caused dad's premature death from a heart attack when he thumbed through the morning mail and saw my registration card for the Socialist Labor Party. I can still hear the echoes of his political screams.

I knew that I had to make some major decisions. A total shift in lifestyle was heading towards me like a locomotive on amphetamines. The idea of moving to Florida floored me as if I had received a roundhouse punch to the gut. How could I trade filthy cement sidewalks and sterile skyscrapers for pristine sandy beaches and palm trees? The thought was intolerable.

# "President's Day weekend turned into the rest of my life."

The new school year was about to commence. I had to return to my home in New York and my job in Connecticut. Mom and dad had regular medical attention now, whether they appreciated it or not, and there was an open line of communication between Hospice and me. I left with a heavy heart. Two weeks after my departure, Hurricanes Ivan and Jeanne hit Florida like Mohammed Ali walloped George Foreman. Those lethal storms almost killed my parents.

Right after Ivan subsided, dad drove to get a newspaper and some cigarettes even though every store in the county was closed. He unwisely navigated over fallen debris, punctured the gas tank, and ran out of gas. Heaven knows how he got back to Atlantis but when he did, dad couldn't remember where he left the car. My father called me in a panic. I played hide-and-seek from up north trying to find that blasted vehicle. A few days later, our empathetic mechanics discovered the Lincoln's leaking body in a Publix parking lot, repaired it, and towed it back to a very grateful Claude and Claudine.

Hurricane Ivan made landfall on September 16, 2004. Florida had no time to recover when deadly Jeanne made her appearance on September 26, 2004. These two natural disasters were the nails in my mother's coffin. She was deathly afraid of violent weather. Our villa had no hurricane protection. My mother shook with fright and swigged vodka as my father and Muffy slumbered through her hours of unmitigated terror.

Christmas came and went in a blur of doctors, medicines, and cleaning agents. My next break was President's Day weekend. By Sunday of that holiday, I made a resolution which greatly impacted our lives. I realized that I couldn't leave my parents for a lengthy period ever again. I told mom how I felt. She cajoled me by whispering that I shouldn't ruin my life. I knew that I would never be able to live with myself if I didn't stay in Florida for "an undetermined amount of time."

It amazed me how quickly I dissolved my life in Manhattan and Wilton and started a completely different existence in Lake Worth. I telephoned Citi-Habitats in New York City and hired an angel of a broker to rent my apartment. A buddy drove my new Honda Civic to the dealership in Connecticut and I sold it back to them. I contacted my compassionate principal and quit my job. I called Jet Blue for a flight home to pack my belongings and a return ticket for the same night. My admirable neighbors helped me sift through my belongings at the speed of light, pack what I needed, store what I didn't, and donate a goodly sum of articles. They also consoled me as I wept through the entire procedure. An understanding friend supervised my furniture's move to a warehouse and the sensational superintendent of my building helped every step of the way.

I was most fortunate to receive the full support of my school's principal, assistant head, the families in my class, and my colleagues. Barely a beat was skipped as I worked closely with administration, my former assistant, and the teacher who took over my position. Each week we were on the telephone for many hours as I coached my associates every step of the way. I prepared individual lesson plans through June for every pupil in the class and wrote each student's mid-winter and spring parent conference summaries plus all of the detailed end-of-the-year reports. I also composed personal notes to the children throughout the remainder of the school year, summer, and fall. Some families still thank me. A few even drop by to say hello when they're in Florida. The work I accomplished from my new home in Atlantis provided me with a certain peace of mind and a paycheck. It also helped maintain my lucidity when the Hospice team informed me that my mother's liver and kidneys were beginning to fail.

## "The good news is your folks are broke."

I never experienced parenthood from a biological point of view but made up for lost time when I cared for my ailing folks. I extend my sincere sympathy to all mothers and fathers whose infants are stricken with colic. Sleep deprivation must be akin to Chinese water torture. In Atlantis I came to understand what "walking into walls" meant. In a state of desperation, I purchased baby monitors for my full grown progeny and hid them near Claude and Claudine's heads. This survival tactic allowed me to doze for a bit while my very soul listened for one or both of them to fall or expire during the night.

Day after day, dad watched TV and smoked as if there was no tomorrow. In reality, there wasn't much of one for him. The love of his life was wasting away before his very eyes. His mind was drying up like a plum in the sun and his lungs heaved as they drew each labored breath. Yet, he moved like a jack rabbit to replace an ice cube in mom's drink.

My waking hours were spent reminiscing with ma. She chuckled as I recounted stories of my adventures with Mrs. Mills, my long time, big breasted, elderly sitter. Each Saturday night in the early 1960's while my parents partied, I was forced to watch The Lawrence Welk Show. For an unbearable hour, the king of "Champagne Music" conducted Mrs. Mills' favorite orchestra. She treasured watching the hideously plastic and conservative performers sing and dance. I tolerated this torture because Mrs. Mills would then endure my favorite science fiction and horror movie program, Chiller Theatre. Sometimes, I was so petrified by the decapitated heads, ghosts, monsters, and zombies crashing about that I channel surfed for momentary relief.

One evening Mrs. Mills and I damn near fell out of our chairs. Guess who we saw in the front row of a heavy weight boxing match at Manhattan's legendary Madison Square Garden? Our eyes almost popped out of our heads as we focused on a gorgeous blonde with her hands crossed at the wrists with palms facing outwardly as if she was bound in a prison cell. This hottie wore a long sleeved black dress with a plunging neckline. A wide collar of layers of white silk trimmed with thin black piping surrounded her countenance. She was evidently blocking droplets of blood splatter. Hemoglobin spurted everywhere while the boxers pummeled each others' heads. Mrs. Mills and I stayed awake until the wee hours of the morning to make sure we hadn't hallucinated. We were flabbergasted as my mother sashayed into the foyer at 3 a.m. with dried plasma all over her gown.

Between administering doses of medicine, assisting trips to the loo, preparing meals, tidying up, and slowly losing my mind, I placed rows of old photographs on top of the clothes in the slightly opened drawers of the highboy next to ma's bed. She relished glancing at portraits of her beloved sister, parents, and friends. Mom bathed in the memories of her long lost mansion, formal galas, the lovely ladies of her bridge club, cotillions, and costume parties. She chuckled as I held up 8 x 10 glossies of her and dad dressed for Halloween as a bullfighter and señorita or a pharaoh and belly dancer.

The Maharaja and Maharani of Yonkers, New York.

My mother recalled how I practically worried her to death on many occasions. As an educator, I had the good fortune to travel around the world. Dad lived vicariously through me. Mom was scared spit less every time I set off for a foreign country until I arrived home. She recommended that I continue living my independent dreams because she never had the courage to do so. Ma offered her special brand of motherly advice, "You don't ever have to get married. If you do, be sure to marry someone who loves you more than you love him." I thought this was a rather callous but astute remark and silently stored the information with a few thousand grains of salt.

Mom frequently asserted she was petrified to depart this life. I reassured her that she would be greeted by everyone she had known and lost. I hinted that dying would be the highlight of her life. I reminded her that everything which was stolen from her would be returned. Our home in Bronxville had been burglarized on three occasions. Each time our abode was vandalized, the robbers turned on all of the lights and left the front door wide open. My unsuspecting mother pictured that a considerate friend had planned three different surprise parties only to be staggered by the fact her home had been ransacked and her treasures stolen.

The grand larcenies persisted. Years later when my parents came to visit me at my apartment in Boston, Massachusetts, their vehicle was broken into and their luggage was taken. I remember how ma cried, "My Arlene Francis diamond heart that Pops gave me is gone!" While dad attended business meetings, a fuming and fearless Claudine dragged me through unwholesome alleyways perpendicular to Boylston Street and interviewed homeless people as to where thieves fenced hot items. We found two pieces of her empty luggage behind a hotel but no necklace.

Little by little, mom and dad had their riches stripped from them. Our life in Florida was an illusion. I lived from hand to mouth without a cent to spare. I rented my apartment in New York City to a string of occupants but my mortgage and tenant's fee did not provide me with a profit. My parents owned a cozy villa and received medical attention. Thank God for Medicare. Still, Claude and Claudine's Social Security checks barely covered their expenses. There was very little money remaining in dad's Smith Barney portfolio. In short, my folks and I were close to being penniless. Once again, Hospice stepped in to the rescue. A social worker was dispatched to our home. Paperwork was completed. A formal announcement was made, "The good news is your folks are broke." With that business settled, a steady stream of aides, nurses, doctors, various professionals, deliveries of medicines, and truckloads of equipment were delivered to our house.

In less than two weeks after my decision to reside in Atlantis, my mother's health declined to such a degree that she had to be lifted into a wheelchair in order to leave her bedroom. Ma's shapely legs were unrecognizable. She donned an uncharacteristic pastel pink and blue flannel full length bathrobe to keep warm. Mom had morphed into the exact image of her own mother. On March 1$^{st}$ ma requested a beverage on the rocks and to be rolled by dad onto the patio where they had entertained themselves for close to five years. My mother proclaimed she wished to venture outside to see the picturesque Floridian sky and our subtropical garden one last time. Dad remarked she'd be fine soon and not to worry. Mom looked him straight in the eye and somehow mustered the strength to holler, "Get with the program, Claude. I'm dying!" This profound statement shut us all up for a solid thirty minutes.

# Part III: "I can't believe it actually happened to me."

## Chapter 13

### "I'll kill myself on the bar if you don't seat thirty people right now!"

Regrettably, my parents were serious lifelong racists. It was the ultimate height of irony when an extremely tall, dignified, and handsome Haitian priest dressed in flowing white robes administered the Last Rites to my mother. Two nurses, each armed with syringes of morphine and tranquilizers, stood at a respectful distance from her bed. My father was in a deep state of shock as he gazed upon his fading wife of fifty-four years. I rocked mom in my arms and verbally attempted to guide her to the proverbial light at the end of the tunnel. Dad insisted I "stop the crap." I ignored him and hopefully ushered Claudine Cecelia Kennedy Seibert into the arms of her awaiting loved ones at 10:40 p.m. on Wednesday, March 2, 2005.

After the morticians took ma on her final midnight ride, dad and I collapsed in two patio chairs and stared at the glowing constellations. We chose an especially large bright star and decided it was my mother gazing down upon us. I searched night after night to find her up in the sky. I asked mom to help me continue on the demanding path I had chosen.

Many years ago ma made it perfectly clear that she wanted to be laid to rest in a pink granite mausoleum. She despised snakes, worms, and insects. Mom thought cremation was distasteful. I guess she thought it might muss her hair. Dad and

I made a pact when I was an adolescent. We wanted to be flash fried when we died. We snickered that my mother would attempt to keep us alive by any means available if we were brain dead. We envisioned mom planting our heads in one of her flower boxes and watering us like some demonic gardener as we lingered in a bodiless state for decades.

On March 3rd my father definitively announced he was going to take my deceased mother to New York and arrange her wake, funeral, and burial by himself. That would have been a truly amazing feat because he couldn't walk around the block and find his way back home. I calmly began my investigation of the world of thieves known as undertakers. For hours I let my fingers do the walking through the <u>Yellow Pages</u> with a calculator by my side. I figured the entire ordeal of shipping mom to The Big Apple and interring her in the most inexpensive pine coffin would cost well over $10,000. Of course, this tidy sum didn't include the cost of a pink tomb suitable for Zsa Zsa Gabor.

Dad quickly agreed to alter his master plan and allowed me to commandeer ma's funeral. I found a seemingly pleasant Catholic Church in Lake Worth less than ten minutes away. I gathered my parents' address books and contacted every person on each tattered page. Dad spoke with the majority of his old friends and was comforted by their condolences and outpourings of love and admiration for mom. Promises of enormous wreaths of pink flowers and flights to Florida filled our hearts. I hired an organist and a choir singer, paid my "donation" to one of St. Luke's priests, sent out the directions and time of the ceremony to dozens of people, prepared a tender eulogy, and headed to the funeral home to pick up mom's ashes and multiple copies of her death certificate.

As I left the miserable parlor, I couldn't freaking believe that I was carrying my mother in a rather heavy, small, cardboard cube. I gently placed her in the passenger's seat of the Lincoln and placed a pair of her oversized sunglasses on the box. No matter how hard you try to do your best, when a parent dies on your shift you feel guilty. I apologized to her and bawled all the way home. I positioned mom on the top shelf of her closet alongside her fashionable high heels. It was somehow comforting to have her nearby even if she had been incinerated.

I double-checked my finalized plans with the church and drove to a popular restaurant which my parents frequented. The Atlantis Grill is conveniently situated just a few minutes from our home and a u-turn away from St. Luke's. I thought it would be impossible for anyone to get lost en route from the church to lunch after the funeral. I introduced myself to the grill's maître d' and willingly accepted his expression of sympathy for my family's loss. We discussed in vivid detail possible seating arrangements and the estimated cost of a luncheon and open bar for at least thirty people. We agreed I'd pay with my Bank of America Visa card. I left believing my parents would be proud and satisfied with the preparations I made for mom's farewell party. I didn't realize that the moron, who I spent a half an hour with, thought I was at the grill for the sole reason of listening to myself talk. Unbeknownst to me, he failed to enter my private gathering for thirty in the establishment's computer.

On the morning of my mother's funeral, I slipped dad a low dose of Ativan which is used to treat anxiety and depression. I wanted to down about eighty of them myself but knew I had to deliver the eulogy and co-host ma's final get-together. The organist said the church had never looked so beautiful. There were rows of magnificent floral arrangements. Some were five feet tall. We left many of them behind at the church's request and brought a dozen home. A sensitive friend put together a photo album of all the flowers for dad to peruse.

I made it through the eulogy and drove the Lincoln full of dad's buddies to the grill. A procession of cars followed us south on Congress Avenue. We all parked and looked forward to drowning our sorrows and eating a fortifying meal. I was shocked when the maître d' discreetly informed me that he had reservations for a full house and couldn't possible seat my party. I asked him to step away from the crowd and discuss the situation with me. I whispered in his ear in a very low and psychotic tone, "I'll kill myself on the bar if you don't seat thirty people right now!" He cautiously stepped back and walked into the kitchen. A flurry of waiters suddenly appeared. The maître d' opened a door on the south wall of the restaurant. The servers huddled for a few moments and began inviting the funeral goers into a private party room. Dad beamed and I praised God.

My father was genuinely touched to be with his cronies again. He came alive for the first time in ages because he was surrounded by love and laughter like the old days. Dad actually smiled, talked, smoked, ate, and drank the entire afternoon. His sudden behavior swing was a full blown miracle in my eyes. March 9th, 2005 marked the end of an era but it also provided some indication of hope for the future.

# "God, no, the rinse cycle!"

Hope turned out to be my intermittent and fickle companion during the next eighteen months. My mother may have been broken by the loss of her mansion on the hill but Claude was pulverized by the loss of Claudine. Grieving is a vitally important psychological process. Dad locked up his intense sorrow as if it were gold bullion at Fort Knox. I never held back tears when they made an unheralded appearance. I broke down at the grocery store if I spotted ma's favorite dessert, key lime pie, on the conveyer belt of the checkout line. I dissolved into a puddle by merely glancing at a box of Swiss Miss Hot Chocolate which my father practically ingested intravenously. My heartache for mom, dad, and my pathetic little life was all encompassing. Therefore, I deduced, "Who the hell cares if I'm weeping as I drag my tired ass down the soup aisle at Publix?" I always felt better by the time I hit the poultry section.

Excluding Cornish hens, turkeys, and chickens, mom adored birds. She ingeniously reproduced likenesses of them in her needlepoint creations. Ma also covered her handmade decoupage wooden pocketbooks with a variety of feathered friends. Robust red cardinals always commanded prominent positions in her artwork.

My mother was thrilled when an occasional scarlet beauty made an appearance in our backyard in Atlantis. The morning after she died, I was pleased to hear one singing. I scampered out onto the patio and found the talkative fellow just a few feet away perched in our grapefruit tree. I whistled to him and we "spoke" for at least five minutes. In my crumbled mind I prayed the cardinal was really mom communicating to me that she was alright. After my discussion with that captivating bird, I walked to my bedroom at the front of the house. As I glanced out my window, I was amazed to see him flying around to the front of the villa and nestling in the ficus hedges across the street. The cardinal remained there for a long time and seemed to be watching me. For many mornings after our initial encounter, I began my day with a ritualistic chat with my new buddy, Big Red.

I often took dad and Muffy on leisurely golf cart rides so we could all breathe some fresh air. A trio of cardinals often swooped directly in front of us as we drove around Atlantis. At least one of the species made almost daily appearances in my life for close to two years. Those beautiful red birds showed up less and less as I psychologically healed from my losses. Today, if I spot a cardinal I still become excited and cheer, "That's my mom!" It doesn't matter if I'm alone or not.

I always kept busy as a bee in the villa so I wouldn't lose my marbles. Being the companion of a person who rarely spoke was very difficult. I discovered that sorting my folks' hundreds of photographs made me feel close to my mother in spite of her absence. I sent a thank you note for a heavenly flower arrangement, a copy of her eulogy, and a packet of specially selected photos in a large manila envelope to my parents' closest friends.

I made piles of pictures and laid them in a time line beginning with Claude and Claudine's courtship through their move to Florida. Mom's bridal photos which were taken in a studio were spectacular. The actual wedding pictures were most disappointing. Dad explained that the photographer arrived at the church in a highly intoxicated state. He captured the images of ladies' derrières quite well but everyone else including the bride and groom were out of focus. My hot tempered Irish grandfather almost killed the lush.

Dad easily recalled events that took place over fifty years ago but couldn't recollect what he'd eaten for breakfast. Luckily, his eyes were excellent. My father was able to read the newspaper without glasses at the age of seventy-eight. In order to make life easier for us, I typed breakfast, lunch, and dinner menus for him. Each collection of edible options listed his favorite foods and beverages. He simply ordered as if he were in a restaurant. The visiting nurses were impressed with my scheme to help dad feel less frustrated. My father enjoyed each meal and could refer to his menus when he wanted to jog his memory as to what he requested.

Living with people you love and watching them slip away is heartbreaking. Keen observation skills, intuition, creativity, and repeatedly attempting to achieve a goal in a variety of ways come into play on a daily basis. Sickly people of any age do not always readily accept the fact that walking sticks, wheelchairs, and commodes for the handicapped will make their lives easier.

It was clear that my father's right hip was starting to fail. He refused to use a cane or walker. Dad hugged a wall as he limped forward or grabbed onto me. He was a large man and I couldn't hold him up any longer. One night in a dream, I envisaged a trail of chairs. When I awakened the next morning, I arranged all of the readily available high-backed, wrought iron, dining room, and Florida Room chairs along the paths dad travelled in the house. Chairs were lined up from his bed to the middle of the living room and veered to the left to his recliner in front of the television. Other chairs continued to the right and out the front door to his smoking center in the carport. The Hospice nurses asked what the heck I was doing with the convolution of seats but wholeheartedly approved as dad proudly shuffled towards them without human assistance.

As the months slowly passed, my father's lower calves and feet began to turn fire engine red with cellulitis. He refused to immerse his feet in Epsom salts to reduce the swelling. Soaking thin terry cloth hand towels in the recommended solution and attaching them to the affected areas with safety pins worked wonders. The only problem with this method is the towels have to be changed quite often. As a primary caretaker I always felt like a hamster on speed. I'd figure out a semi-suitable solution to one problem and another dilemma would arise instantaneously.

Eventually, dad needed to begin Coumadin injections to thin his blood. I'm not squeamish so that wasn't a problem. The possibility of bleeding to death was less of a drawback to my father than the mandatory directive to stop shaving. Dad was still a handsome gentleman even though he was close to eighty. Within a few weeks, my clean-cut Claude looked like a dejected Santa Claus. I did a double take every time I looked at him. Where was Ricky Ricardo?

Dad's first birthday without mom approached. What could I get him? His stylish loafers wouldn't fit anymore and his favorite belt was practically in shreds. I purchased a navy and white striped pair of rubber flip-flops which fastened with Velcro across the instep. Father cherished his new belt from Casual Male XL and moseyed around in uncharacteristic footwear on his special day. He ate a favorite meal of an Italian meatball wedge and Breyer's vanilla ice cream for dessert. It was a simple, quiet, and melancholy celebration.

It had only been six months since I moved to Florida but it felt like six years. I needed to vent my fears and frustrations. I confided in a Hospice nurse because I was positive she knew how important it is to provide emotional support to caregivers. She informed me Hospice has three levels of guidance for adults. I took advantage of all of them. First, I attended three meetings at Hospice Headquarters with a group of grieving individuals. A counselor was present and invited people to share their stories. There was no pressure to participate. Some just listened. Others wailed with grief as they told their tales of woe. Any way you looked at it, catharsis was the theme.

At the second level, I met with twelve other individuals who were in similar situations once a week for a period of three months. A counselor guided our discussions. Treasured photographs and memories were shared. Bonds were created amongst people that continued outside of the four walls of Hospice Headquarters. True and lasting friendships developed.

The third level consisted of private counseling sessions at my home for eighteen months. As I became stronger, the weekly sessions lessened to once a month then once every six weeks until I regained my sanity, got a job, sold the corpse of a Lincoln, and disinfected and painted every square inch of the villa. When I completed my counseling sessions, my mental and emotional savior informed me that I was considered a "lifelong member." That meant I may rejoin Hospice's counseling program at no cost at any time in the future if I "experienced a relapse." Now that's community service at its finest. To this day I make modest donations to Hospice a few times a year. I also made provisions in my will for Hospice to receive the balance of my estate following my cremation. I am a proud and grateful member of the Hospice Legacy Society.

Even after I began counseling, I needed to escape from the house for short periods of time to clear my head. I made sure dad and Muffy were safe and had plenty of food and drink. I drove to the post office, CVS, Home Depot, Publix, or the hardware store as if they were expensive European getaways. One day when I was feeling especially fragile, I decided to be wild and carefree. I had not been to the Mobil gas station's carwash in a while. I donned a shabby black dress, fuchsia flip-flops, and dark sunglasses to hide my bloodshot eyes. All I wanted was a little rest and relaxation in a dark box as the car got cleaned. As the pink, yellow, and blue suds began their slimy journey all over the Lincoln, I realized that the lousy sun roof leaked. I scrambled back and forth in the front seat like a crazed rat in a maze trying to avoid the bubbles. My nerves were shot and I cried like a two year old. The damn slippery soap finally subsided and then I thought, "God, no, the rinse cycle!" I was hysterical as I drove out of that wretched, gigantic, washing machine.

When I turned onto a busy Military Trail to head back home after my misadventure, I heard a small explosion. The back left tire blew. Now, I was soaked and furious. I crawled along the road hoping not to damage the rim of the wheel. Suddenly, a siren screamed behind me. Good God Almighty, a State Trooper insisted that I pull over. He took one look at me and asked, "What happened to you, lady? Is this your car?" I explained my misfortune and inquired if he thought anyone would willingly drive this heap unless they were forced to do so. The sheriff stepped back, removed his mirrored sunglasses, bent over slightly, and began laughing so hard that he got me howling too. The officer was most helpful and allowed me to follow him to my faithful mechanics. I dried out in the sun while they changed my tire. I gladly returned home to my two charges. I didn't possess the courage or emotional strength to venture out of the house again for quite some time.

# "Can you sell this mink coat for me?

My mother was emotionally attached to the dust on her possessions. She wouldn't dispose of a toothbrush even if Ayatollah Khomeini ordered her to do so. The only reason my father and I didn't have to peddle matches on street corners was for the fact that I sold ninety percent of my parents' belongings. After Claudine died, Claude didn't give a hoot about anything. That was one of the advantages of mom passing before dad. At first I asked his permission to hawk, let's say, the living room furniture. My father blindly nodded his consent, sipped his fifty-third cup of hot cocoa, smoked his ninety-seventh cigarette, and watched some more television as trucks drove away with a roomful of his belongings. I would then run to the bank and pray over the deposit hoping that Jesus would perform a "Loaves and Fishes" miracle on our earnings.

Mom's Social Security check discontinued when she died. Therefore, dad's income diminished significantly. I was shocked at how inconsiderate our government is to spouses on a fixed income. How could my father continue to exist at the same decent standard of living? I also had to scrounge for the money to pay my Cobra insurance bill each month. My horseback riding ceased the day I arrived in Florida because it was too expensive to pursue. Hospice also recommended that I discontinue my much-loved hobby because there would be no one to take care of dad if I got injured. Hospice's assumption was correct. I would have broken my neck the second I mounted a polo pony because I couldn't concentrate on anything except my father and our financial survival.

I started to peddle everything we owned that wasn't nailed down. A trustworthy friend had procured many different types of business connections in Florida. He set up meetings for me with legitimate buyers. In the mornings I unloaded gold, platinum, and diamonds at the dining room table for cold cash. In the afternoons I got rid of rifles, pistols, and ammunition. Auctioneers visited the house. They examined every article we owned as they rummaged through pieces of art, drawers, and cabinets. Vans, private cars, and pick-up trucks removed remnants of my parents' past on a daily basis.

One night I attended an auction in Delray and observed as my family's possessions were sold off and carted away. I was amazed how people's prized personal effects left their hands forever with one swing of a mallet. After three hours I stumbled to the dilapidated Lincoln in a daze. I heard my name called by an appraiser. He congratulated me and handed over a hefty check. I smiled, thanked him for his patient assistance, and drove back to Atlantis feeling like a prostitute who had a bad night.

My marketing didn't stop there. I transported mom's extravagant costume jewelry, vintage handbags, shoes, and clothing along with my grandmother's multiple pairs of opera length kid gloves, tortoise shell cigarette holders and cases with matching lighters plus her retro cat eye sunglasses, and hundreds of handmade tablecloths, serviettes, and cocktail napkins in every color and size to a variety of consignment stores. I called each shop every week to ascertain what did and did not sell. If I couldn't move merchandise at one place, I rotated it to another store.

Ma's mink pill box hats were eaten up like candy. The most difficult piece to unload was her mink coat. I dragged that furry beast around for ages and was prepared to ditch it in a canal when I finally received a sizable check from a scrapheap in Greenacres Mall. What I could not leave with an auctioneer or a consignment store, I sold by lot or donated to the Vietnam Veterans of America. The Vets picked up contributions at our front door and left a blank certificate for me to fill in and hand over to dad's accountant for a tax deduction. Dad's cashmere sports jackets and coats, business shirts and suits, parkas, snow boots, and hundreds of silk ties plus mom's modern casual daywear met this honorable fate.

It took months to sufficiently empty the villa in order to make room for my belongings which were shipped from storage in Manhattan to Florida. My furniture consisted of prized pieces formerly owned by my mother and grandmother. I loaned half of it to a close friend and her fiancé who needed furnishings for their home in upstate New York. The other half was delivered to Atlantis by a den of clumsy thieves who destroyed or stole gilded mirrors, antique tables, sets of china, and chairs. As providence would have it, all of mom's smashed belongings wouldn't have fit in the villa anyway. After that mind-bending experience with the bandits who disguised themselves as movers, I developed a new theory concerning any article of mine that was lost, stolen, or broken: I'm simply not supposed to possess it anymore, period.

## "Would you care for some extra tanks of oxygen?

Our finances continued to dwindle in spite of my entrepreneurial efforts. I sold my jewelry and depleted my coffers. My mantra was, "What the heck am I going to do?" A trip to the mailbox was similar to a root canal. I couldn't stand the sight of another bill. One morning I discovered a letter for me with a return address I did not recognize. I opened it, gasped, and collapsed in the driveway. There was a check written out to yours truly in the amount of ten thousand dollars. Tears of joy streamed down my face. I raced to tell dad of our miracle made of paper and then floored the Lincoln to the bank. The teller even twitched in disbelief.

Our luck changed for the better in the blink of an eye. A sympathetic and saintly parent from my school in Connecticut was our champion. Her incredible generosity enabled me to fix the roof and golf cart; purchase a new water heater, clothes washer, microwave oven, patio door, and tires and seat covers for the Lincoln; remove the nauseating white carpet in the villa; and install two toilets for the handicapped, kitchen faucets that actually worked, and tasteful yet inexpensive white tile throughout most of the house.

I knew my novel sense of security was fleeting at best. Therefore, I began computer lessons to improve my typing skills. I also researched teaching positions, home schooling opportunities, and part time secretarial jobs within a ten mile radius of Atlantis. I even considered being a mock juror which paid ten dollars an hour. Fortunately, I landed a job from 9 a.m. to 3 p.m. instructing three students of Middle Eastern descent who were Jehovah's Witnesses. Their parents didn't approve of any schools in the entire state. I became their educational guide for a season and left with a fistful of dollars every afternoon. Whenever I had a spare moment, I tweaked my résumé and called up north for my employment records. Thank God Florida and New York practice reciprocity which means I wouldn't have to take an examination for a license unless I taught out of my field.

Whenever I arrived home from my new teaching position, a Hospice nurse inquired after my health because I emerged from the car sweating like a marathon runner. With a concerned look she placed her hand on my brow or cheek and sighed. I realized that I looked like a bloated lobster each time I exited the Lincoln. Dad's death trap had no air conditioning. It reached at least 105 degrees inside that black oven in the summer. The back windows were sealed shut due to burned out motors. It was also impossible to lock the doors of his hunk of junk but no one in their right mind would steal it since the radio, defogger, and sun roof didn't work either. I periodically attempted to remove some of the deep dents in the Lincoln. I stood in its trunk with a sledge hammer wrapped in a beach towel and banged out as many furrows as possible in its worn-out body.

I slowly came to truly appreciate southern hospitality. First and foremost, the Hospice community helped my family in innumerable ways. Neighbors, proprietors, my hair dresser, mechanics, cab drivers, accountants, the handsome UPS guy, handy men, landscapers, and the vast collection of people who delivered medical supplies to our villa were always ready with a smile, a helping hand, a comforting comment, or a generous gesture. Can you believe my lawyer in Boca Raton expressed that he hadn't come across someone in my particular circumstances and cut my fees by a third? Even the chap who delivered oxygen in case there was a power failure took me to the side and whispered, "Would you care for some extra tanks, ma'am? No one has to know. You'll feel more at ease if there's a hurricane." My mother's closet no longer contained stylish high heels. It now held enough gas to blow us all to kingdom come.

## **"Shall we call her Incognito?"**

One of the most insidious aspects of dad's dementia was that it robbed him of his present and future but left his past intact. I often felt my father and I were trapped on the same ship which was lost at sea. Unfortunately, it was sinking due to an excess of sorrow, steroids, nebulizers, and oxygen tanks. The biggest difference between our journeys was that his was going to end sooner than mine. The highlight of our voyage was a comfy recliner that magically lifted a seated person to a standing position. It bolstered our respective spirits and spinal columns every day and night.

My father and I shared a fair amount of unusual memories. Dad always enjoyed recollecting his experiences on the water. We grinned as we recalled one wintry day at a marina in Greenwich when he proudly purchased his Bayliner cruiser. Dad bargained with the dock master and walked away with a bill of sale for his dream come true. First he wanted to christen it, *The Three C's*. I warned him how depressing it would be to eventually rename his vessel, *The Two C's*, and then, *One Damn Lonely C*. He agreed to keep her original name, *Incognito*. I thought it was a fabulously sexy name and willingly hopped onboard given the opportunity.

Dad, Muffy II, and I stole out to sea for a couple of hours whenever I visited on summer weekends. My mother wasn't steady enough on her feet to join us. She was content to polish her nails and sip a cocktail knowing her "kidlets" were amusing themselves in a nautical fashion. I packed a picnic, some cold beer, and a couple of dog biscuits. We cruised passed the Westchester Country Club and remarked how fortunate we were to have romped with our friends for all those years. We also explored small uninhabited islands which was illegal but exhilarating. Sometimes we just dropped anchor, stared at the water, and blissfully disregarded the fact that the matriarch of our miniature dynasty was slowly disappearing.

As I look back upon the events of that day, it was evident my father suffered from dementia even then. I didn't possess enough knowledge at the time to diagnose his quiet forgetfulness and odd clueless behavior. Our final escapade in the Atlantic Sound was rather dismal. It was a warm and clear day as dad and I inspected the progress of the renovations of older mansions as we hugged the Connecticut coastline. After our investigation was complete, we decided to head back to our marina. That's when we ran out of gas. I was grateful that we were near a massive twelve foot stone jetty which belonged to an estate that was being remodeled.

The water was choppy as we drifted towards the rocky structure. I hastily put out the bumpers in an attempt to protect *Incognito* from crashing against an unforgiving wall. My father just sat there not knowing what to do. I raced around like a gerbil on a mission in my navy blue linen dress and matching suede high heeled mules. It dawned on me that if I climbed to the top of the jetty, I could tie up *Incognito* and dad and Muffy would be safe while I got help. I balanced on the deck alongside the cabin and leaped onto one of the craggy walls like Spider-Man's well-dressed cousin as dad held on to a rocky protrusion with a hook. The jagged placement of rocks acted like steps. I reached my destination and rolled onto my stomach as my father hurled lines to me to make the boat fast.

I was still on my belly in sand up to my ears when I heard a male voice inquire if I cared for some assistance. Of course I needed aid and a stiff shot of absinthe! The gentleman turned out to be the architect at the site. Thomas made sure dad and the Bayliner were out of harm's way and accompanied me to his trailer where he called the water police to tow our craft. Tom then escorted me to the fuel dock where I met dad, Muffy, and the cops. My father and I apologized for the inconvenience we had caused, thanked everyone, and returned to *Incognito's* mooring. After an interminable day, we left the marina. Dad drove our sorry sailor butts home to mom where an extra-long cocktail hour ensued.

## "I saved your father's life a year ago."

One sultry Floridian evening as a powerful storm brewed, I noticed an incredibly skinny, highly unattractive, pointy nosed dog trembling in our carport. I went to investigate and seated myself in dad's smoking chair. After one crack of mighty thunder, the pathetic pooch glued himself to my calves. I escorted him into my bedroom and introduced the coward to an aloof Muffy. After frisking the shaking pup, I decided to contact the Atlantis police. Within moments, an enormous officer came to my assistance. He noticed a tiny phone number on one of the animal's tags. Merlin was an expensive Italian Greyhound with a microchip concealed under his pelt. I couldn't help but shake my head as I gazed at the gargantuan cop, chubby poodle, and emaciated vagrant. I contemplated how dad was sleeping soundly as I ran a lost and found service.

I called the owner who happened to be on her way home to Atlantis from Orlando. It took her over two hours to pick up her stray pooch. During this time, Merlin fell hopelessly in love with the Muffster. It was touching to watch the canine romance develop. Finally, an absolutely enchanting, pale, tall, redhead arrived and explained that Merlin was her father's dog. After numerous apologies and expressions of gratitude, Lillian introduced herself with a story that left me speechless.

"It's odd that you did me a favor tonight. I saved your father's life a year ago." Lillian described how she, her mother, Esther, and her sister, Adelaide, were driving along Lantana Road which is parallel to Atlantis. Esther, who just happens to be a nurse, spotted a large black sedan on the side of the thoroughfare. The driver was clearly in a state of distress. He was hunched over the steering wheel. God knows how many apathetic people sped by my semi-conscious father that day. Lillian, Esther, and Adelaide managed to get Claude home, administer his medications, and deliver him into the bed of a startled but appreciative Claudine. Merlin could have knocked me over with a rawhide chew toy after hearing this moving tale of mercy. I was astounded how three total strangers made an everlasting impact on my family. I thanked Lillian and bid goodnight to Muffy's new suitor.

The next day Lillian returned to our villa to see dad once again. It was as if Nancy Reagan sauntered into our Florida Room. His eyes lit up like twinkling stars. From that moment on, Lillian visited my father regularly. As she spoke of religion and salvation, dad taught her how to play checkers and legitimately won almost every game. She, in turn, acquainted him with Texas Hold'em Poker. This silken haired seraph took my father on golf cart rides and accompanied him to lunch at The Palm Beach Kennel Club to watch the dog races, and to his last notable outing at The International Polo Club in Wellington. Lillian breathed life into a dying man's broken heart. She was a whisper of spring to him. I am convinced Lillian's warmth and kindness kept dad alive. Her visits also preserved my sanity.

Dad was still able to take care of his personal needs with minimal assistance. I trained him how to eat and drink from the labeled containers on the folding table next to his lounger. The television kept him occupied when Lillian or a nurse weren't present. I administered his meds in the mornings and evenings. Everything was relatively manageable until Hospice announced that it was almost time to dismiss my father from their care. He was their prized patient "who survived the longest, one and one-half years." I couldn't believe my ears.

I knew dad would be thrilled that "those people" wouldn't be "bothering" him anymore. I decided to break the news at one of my parents' favorite seaside restaurants, the Old Key Lime House. Before lunch we stopped at a nearby charter school so I could drop off my résumé. Just by chance, the principal was at the front desk. I introduced myself and handed her my life in a large manila envelope. Strangely enough, she took the time to peruse my credentials, told me she liked my smile and firm handshake, and hired me on the spot. Lucky for me, she was desperate because a fifth grade teacher had just resigned to pursue a better paying position. That should have been a hint right there. However, I was delirious with gratefulness.

Shortly thereafter, I began working for slave's wages in a ratty one story building that used to be owned by <u>The National Enquirer</u>. Every day freight trains, just yards from my classroom, rattled the windows in their frames. This was a far cry from my immaculate Montessori classrooms on the Upper West Side of Manhattan and a pristine suburb of Connecticut. I had almost two weeks to prepare for my new students. From the get-go there were countless trainings and so much red tape that I labored until late at night and at least twelve hours on Sundays.

My new class of eager public school students arrived on Wednesday, August 16, 2006. I came home from school that day and immediately sensed there was something wrong. Dad was very groggy and in bed. He indicated that he desired to smoke. His listless body was draped across mine as I dragged him onto the patio. That was my father's last cigarette.

# "The Pope would be ashamed of you!"

Even though Hospice was ready to dismiss dad, I called and pleaded for help. A nurse arrived within an hour, was horrified after examining him, and demanded that Hospice headquarters dispatch a doctor and more nurses to the villa. My father had a restful night. The next morning the medical team convinced me to go to school. Dad was weak but able to speak by Thursday afternoon. I returned to school on Friday morning only to receive a call at noon. There was a "medical emergency" at home. I had a flashback of ma and me speeding through the streets on Christmas Eve to her father almost forty years ago. This time I was the one driving towards death.

That same afternoon Lillian came by for an impromptu visit and was accompanied by Esther and Adelaide. Esther never came to Atlantis in order to avoid seeing her former husband. It was an uncanny coincidence that all three ladies arrived at the house when my father and I most needed them. I called Gert, our helpful neighbor, to say goodbye to dad. She brought a dozen blood red roses.

Lillian, her mother, and her sister greeted my father, sat at the foot of his bed, and began singing to him. For hours on end their angelic harmonies filled dad's bedroom. We all sang "Happy Birthday" to him even though it was eleven days before the actual event. I held my father in my arms and whispered that his early present would be to caress his beloved Claudine again. Lillian, Esther, and Adelaide sang "Amazing Grace" as Claude Decker Seibert drew his last breath at 6 p.m. on Friday, August 18th, 2006.

When the nurses, morticians, and my dear friends left, I automatically scooped up Muffy and headed for the patio to inspect the familiar layout of constellations. I felt like my body and soul had been pounded by invisible mortar as I flopped into the same chair I sank into after my mother died. I was startled to find a star just below hers. I never noticed that surprising sparkler in all these months. It wasn't as bright or as beautiful as mom's, but it was steady and strong just like dad. It was as if the second star miraculously appeared when my father disappeared from Earth. I imagined that the two stars were companions in the glittering sky.

After a few hours, I took my musings a step further. I was relieved that Claude and Claudine were together again. After all, I could see them with my very own eyes.

I grieved over the weekend and made the decision that it would be too brain damaging to organize dad's funeral during the following week. I had to wait for his cremation and death certificate plus I had to think of my new students. It would have been enormously disruptive for them to lose their new teacher at the beginning of the school year. I knew that it would be the best therapy for me to be around youngsters who were full of life and energy.

I purchased the same, highly polished, hollow, brass cube which my godmother and ma's best friend, Suzette, had generously bought for my mother's earthly remains. I didn't want to take any chances this time around. I made arrangements once again at St. Luke's Church and The Atlantis Grill almost three weeks in advance. I scheduled dad's funeral for Saturday, September 9th, at 10 a.m. The luncheon in his honor was set for noon.

There were no problems with The Atlantis Grill affair. However, the secretary at St. Luke's began harassing me to "reconsider" the day of my father's funeral because "a very important bishop from Miami" wanted dad's time slot for his cousin's funeral. I had already informed our friends of the solemn ceremony. The clerical worker's reason boiled my blood so I told her that it was not possible. Priests called and demanded that I change my father's funeral date. I held my ground and stated, "We are all created as equals. I don't understand why my dad doesn't rate in your eyes."

On the appointed Saturday I arrived at St. Luke's thirty minutes in advance to speak with the organist and choir singer and to make sure that all the flowers were placed in a pleasant manner on the altar. There was nowhere to park. I had to squeeze the Lincoln into a cramped space in the adjoining school's lot. There were lines of black limousines and chauffeurs in black suits. I clutched dad in his small brass box in one hand. In the other, I carried a stunning photograph of Claude and Claudine in a sterling frame as they attended a gala event. Dad looked smashing in a tuxedo and mom wore a silver cocktail dress with matching stilettos and a short, white mink jacket.

Every pew was packed. My organist and very pregnant choir singer greeted me in the vestibule with long faces. They led me to a small chapel. To my disbelief, all of my father's floral arrangements were sitting in pews as if they were attending a funeral for a sacred Royal palm tree. As dad's friends arrived, I ushered them into the cramped area to wait until the bishop's niece's funeral concluded. We inhaled putrid incense and cursed the selfish hierarchy of the Catholic Church.

My nerves were frayed. I was livid because the so-called men of God had disregarded my wishes. No one at the church offered to assist me as I lugged all of dad's gorgeous flowers to the altar. A scrawny priest finally made an appearance and began the service one hour late. This complete idiot had the nerve to announce at Communion that he would appreciate it if "no Jews came to receive the body of Christ." I almost stormed the altar and strangled the ignorant pipsqueak. After the ceremony another member of the clergy had the gonads to ask me for the customary $300 "donation" for dad's funeral. I suggested that the larcenous low life pay me for the humiliation he caused my family. As I handed him the money, I glared at the pious fraud and seethed, "The Pope would be ashamed of you." He cashed my check the following week.

I led the procession of cars to the restaurant. All I could think about was vodka. After inhaling two Cosmopolitans, I enjoyed a tasty luncheon with my father's comrades. We reminisced about Claude and Claudine and toasted them. People congratulated me for delivering a touching eulogy. I admitted that I was in a trance when I composed and delivered it.

Quite a few of mom and dad's friends were considerably older than my folks. When we bid our farewells I couldn't help but wonder how much longer they would be alive. I dropped that depressing thought like a hot stone. I still had to figure out what to do with the vestiges of my parents but that decision would have to wait for another day.

# Chapter 14

## "You've been through so much; I'll give you the urn."

One of my next door neighbors named Georgia decided that it was high time to move to a retirement home but desired to maintain her villa and car in Atlantis. She asked me to watch over her pristine Coupe de Ville Cadillac and occasionally look in on her house. No problema! I cherished driving that unblemished, respectable, and highly polished vehicle. Thank God her automobile was at my disposal because tooling around in dad's hunk of junk was akin to driving a time bomb. The Lincoln continued to deteriorate. It sunk lower to the ground each day. During its last visit to my trusty mechanics, Moe and Essie chimed, "We have good news and bad news. The good news is that you're still alive. The bad news is the gas tank scrapes the road every time you go over a bump. You are a moving Molotov cocktail." They rationalized the suspension system was basically non-functional. That's why I looked like a Spanish gangster's moll in a funky low rider!

A few weeks later, I ventured to the carport and discovered that the underside of the Lincoln was less than an inch from the floor. I gingerly sat in the driver's seat. When I attempted to put the car in drive, the gear shift wouldn't budge. That was it. I called about half a dozen towing companies before I found someone willing to deal with the Lincoln's breakdown. A man who appeared to be a tanned cousin of Saint Nicholas arrived to dispose of dad's black metal carcass. It took him a while to fathom how to maneuver my father's heap out of the driveway. Good old St. Nick paid me $125 and dragged away the lethal sedan.

I was surprised at my reaction. I stood in the driveway and wailed. I witnessed sparks from the wreckage as it dug into the road like it was fighting to remain at the villa. I felt like dad's ghost was kicking and screaming because he didn't want to be forgotten. I shook with grief and didn't care if anyone observed. Pride was an emotion of the past. My tank was out of gas.

The Lincoln was history and Claude and Claudine resided in shiny brass cubicles on the top shelf of the master bedroom closet. I greeted them warmly each morning and evening. The thought of my parents leaving Atlantis was unbearable. I needed to carefully plan my next move in order to save myself from any unnecessary distress.

I evoked mom and dad's extensive quest for romantic restaurants by the water. I knew ma loved the sea because I recalled her giggling, "Swimming in the ocean is the quickest way to cure a hangover." I discussed various possibilities with a funeral director in Lake Worth. He patiently explained how a yacht owned by his establishment cruised to a legal distance on alternate Sundays and the crew dispersed ashes. I was guaranteed that my parents' remains would be intermingled before they were set free in the wind. It seemed poetic that my folks would be sprinkled in the mighty Atlantic. I recalled how dad built a small boat from scratch during their courtship. They owned the Bayliner cruiser, *Incognito*, in Connecticut. My folks loved deep sea fishing parties and carousing with their buddies on the open water. I actually felt comfortable planning Claude and Claudine's last swim together for the following weekend.

I sincerely believe in life after death so I felt like an utter fool when I found myself incapable of surrendering my parents' ashes to the funeral director. I couldn't help but think, "What the hell is wrong with me?" as I clutched two heavy cartons of useless dust with a few chunks of bones in them like I was some kid being strong armed into giving up my blanky. I circled like a wounded animal in the room where they showcased coffins. My eyes settled upon the section reserved for urns. I noticed a series of typically insipid ones but then an absolutely divine, spherical, cerulean blue, cloisonné urn came into view.

This petite gem was only two inches wide and three and one-half inches tall. It possessed a handsome domed lid. On one of its sides a pair of graceful swans was portrayed in profile. Their necks curved in such a way that their beaks and breasts touched and formed the shape of a heart. The elegant birds floated on navy water with delicate golden scrolls posing as waves. Opposite the swans there were lotus flowers, an ancient Asian symbol of creation. I was struck by the fact there were three lotuses and imagined that each blossom represented a member of my family. I envisioned some of my parents' ashes resting peacefully in this tasteful little vessel. The director offered to make my wish come true and waived the cost of the miniature jewel. He patted me on the shoulder and stated, "You've been through so much; I'll give you the urn."

Today the swans perch on one of my mother's marble topped side tables next to my Siamese fighting fish in the Florida Room. The fortunate set of gills swims in a fabulous cylindrical vase etched with circular designs which formerly held mom's lavish floral arrangements. I get to see my folks every day and no one is the wiser.

## "We put the "d's" in death and dysfunctional."

Crazed memories surfaced as I trudged through the quagmire of depression after losing my loved ones. I recollected looking up the definition of "urn" in Webster's Dictionary when I was a teen. It simply stated, "Any type of container." My research began one afternoon after school. I was a sophomore at a Catholic penitentiary. I came home to find what I thought was a gallon of paint on the front doorstep. It had a rectangular sticker sloppily pasted at an askew angle on its side. I squinted to read the minuscule words, "Herbert D. Seibert." Holy crap! It was my paternal grandfather. He hadn't been to our home in ages. I placed my incinerated relative in the front hall where my parents would surely notice him.

I was not emotionally impacted by the incident because I never really knew that side of the family. Herb had gone mad, lost a fortune due to his compulsive gambling, broke everyone's heart, and died in a nursing home about ten minutes away in downtown Yonkers. I recalled visiting his vast estate in Scarsdale when I was a kid. My father also took me to see his folks in their handsome apartment on Garth Road in Scarsdale. Dad supported them after my grandfather's scandalous downfall and rented the place until my grandmother passed. I accompanied dad when he called on Herbert a few months before my grandfather died.

Dad casually placed his deceased father's "urn" in the pantry with our food. Mom inquired if he was hinting she should go on a diet. He then wedged Herb next to the encyclopedias and wine goblets in a cherry wood book case in the dining room until we figured out how, when, and where to dispose of him. My parents were broke at the time. They couldn't pay the ridiculous sum for grandpa's interment in the enormous Seibert family plot at Woodlawn Cemetery in the Bronx. Woodlawn is a remarkable burial site that opened in 1863 in the outskirts of Manhattan.

We waited for relatively warm weather, drove south on the Bronx River Parkway, and asked the guard on duty at Woodlawn for a map "to visit our long lost relatives." Ma was dressed in black and played dual roles as decoy and look out. My father and I dug like madmen with trowels from mom's garden. Dad shoved his father in the ground. We stamped on him a few times, threw some pine needles on his fresh grave, wished him well, and got the heck out of there as fast as we could.

Death is never very far away from anyone as much as my mother tried to keep that tidbit of reality hidden from me during my formative years. My grandma owned a charismatic canary named Petey whom I greatly admired. Mom purchased a similar but sickly companion for me. He lived for an abbreviated lifespan in a large cylindrical cage in an upstairs guest bedroom. The Green Room was huge and nippy in the winter. I'm sure my fragile pet perished from consumption. At least the first one did.

I never had the opportunity to develop a substantial relationship with my birds because they kept dying. My mother discovered a yellow, stiff, little body every few weeks and scrambled to purchase another live specimen. She couldn't comprehend that I had developed the mental capability to decipher one feathered creature from another. Ma "didn't want me to experience sadness and death at such a young age" even though I thoroughly scrutinized my deceased acquaintances hours before her daily survival inspection. The poor woman frantically shopped for canaries the entire season until she tired of battling with The Grim Reaper. Mother moved onto more convenient corpses such as goldfish, then turtles, and finally mammals. Fortunately, toy poodles are rather hearty.

Carcasses followed me to Connecticut. Before my parents moved to Florida, they sold their apartment in Greenwich without telling me. Consider the fact that I was jackassing all the way from the Upper West Side of Manhattan to Wilton, Connecticut when my parents lived only a short distance from my school. It seemed life would have been so much easier if I could have taken over their flat. At least ten loathsome hours of commuting time would have vanished from my hectic weekly schedule. My under eye area would have also benefitted from moving further north.

I drove up and down the Hutchison River and Merritt Parkways for close to four years and subsequently renamed the route Road Kill Haven. I frequently arrived at work crying like a baby. Mangled cars, careening emergency vehicles, miles of backed-up traffic, splattered does, dismembered bucks, a grieving goose circling her unconscious gander, turkey feathers spread far and wide, and the strong odor of compressed skunks were just some of the delights I encountered shortly after dawn five days a week. I still flinch if I see a mass in the road when I drive around Palm Beach County. However, I'm pleased to report that it's usually a wad of sod that's flown off a landscaper's truck. Many traffic jams in the Sunshine State have been caused by an apathetic iguana soaking up the heat from the pavement of a congested thoroughfare. Believe me, I'd much rather sit in a line of cars for a lazy lizard in Florida than count corpses in Connecticut.

## "There's a bomb by the jack-o'-lantern."

It doesn't matter if you share bloodlines with Mother Theresa, Mahatma Gandhi, and Pope John XXIII. Every family has its fair share of larcenous lunatics and traces of insanity, avarice, and visions of grandeur. Yet, ancestral documentation reveals that unenviable genetic traits and character weaknesses in some relatives are often counteracted with incredible acts of love, generosity, and compassion by others. History, even on the most personal levels, repeats itself.

Dad was like a broken record. The same song always played on his virtual Victrola. It was called, "How Can I Make My Wife Happy in the Face of Adversity?" For most of his adult life my father couldn't afford to buy trinkets similar to the ones he found in his beloved Cracker Jacks boxes. That didn't stop him from occasionally splurging on baubles which he hoped would please his spouse. Mother adored jewelry. Diamonds, emeralds, and star rubies fascinated her. The only real gems ma ever owned were bestowed upon her after her mother's demise.

During one of many sleepless nights, dad ordered a ring from QVC television shopping channel. "Quality, Value, and Convenience" meant diddlysquat to my mother. You'd have better luck uttering the words, "Let's visit a Harry Winston Salon." Mom loved almost anything that was pink or lavender. So, dad charged a little over $500 to his overused VISA card for a charming pear-shaped amethyst in a 24 carat gold setting.

It was delivered one autumn afternoon by UPS but no one was home. A carton about the size of a softball was deposited next to our ornate Halloween pumpkin near the front door. It remained there for a couple of weeks. Ma noticed the package but never picked it up. After a considerable amount of time had passed, dad inquired if mom had received his televised present. My mother stated that she hadn't but suggested that he fetch the parcel by the decorated squash.

Ma opened it and pretended she was pleased. Alas, it wasn't the Hope Diamond. Dad asked why she never brought the delivery into the house. Mother casually replied, "I wasn't expecting any packages so I assumed it was a bomb." That was a perfect example of logic in Claudine's world. I wondered what her reaction would have been if dad had been blown to pieces. I'm sure ma would have fiercely hunted down the terrorist that detonated her husband and her new ring.

My father would have probably survived the explosion because he was like a cat. Dad surely possessed nine lives. I am convinced that he willed himself to stay alive throughout their fifty-four years of marriage in order to tend to mom when she became ill. The quality of care he provided was highly questionable and downright homicidal at times. Nevertheless, he always tried his best. No wonder I never got married. In my mind, it was safer to take my chances with a poodle rather than someone like my dear old pop.

Before I came to live with my parents in Florida, I visited often. Ma could hardly swallow due to her tracheal disorder. I often watched in disbelief as dad lovingly prepared steak or lamb chops with a side order of vodka for my mother's dinner. It was like he was providing nourishment for a Russian wrestler instead of a good-natured skeleton who ate like a wren. Somehow she managed to live through almost five years of comparable meals. Perhaps it was the potatoes in the vodka that kept her going or maybe it was because they loved each other so much that they just didn't want to part.

## "My jaw hurts; we've been on the phone for five hours."

I honestly believe that you can heal your life if you keep your eyes open and notice some of the blessings that are present all around us. There are dozens of little gifts sprinkled throughout the day. You have to practice to become cognizant of them. Sometimes a meeting is conveniently cancelled so you can finish up your paperwork and go home on time or a specific catalog shows up in the mailbox when you need to order something for your home. When I lived with my folks, I had to look really hard for my boons but they were always there. People also magically entered my life when I needed them the most.

I was a drooling fool as I went to transfer ownership of my parents' home into my name and to file for homestead exemption. It was a momentous day and I couldn't stop sobbing. Mom had rallied for the last time and dad was losing touch with reality with every passing moment. There was a Hospice aide at the house so I decided to take my mind off my troubles and search for tiles to replace the villa's stained carpeting. My face was blotchy and my eyes were swollen. I looked like I had gone a round with Sonny Liston. I was dressed in a typically stunning outfit consisting of a hideous brown shift purchased for pennies at the supermarket and black rubber flip-flops. When I entered a store across from The Property Appraiser's Office, I was so depressed that my aura must have been the color of tar.

As I dragged my sorry ass through the aisles and tried to maintain my focus on flooring, I noticed a handsome sales representative. He approached me and we began talking about everything except tiles for close to an hour. I brought home a few samples to see if they complemented what was already in our villa. I travelled back and forth between the establishment and Atlantis until I settled on an inexpensive but attractive 16" x 16" off-white tile that ended up in three quarters of our abode. I struck a super deal and managed to make a friend as a bonus.

My new buddy resided with his daughter who attended a local college. He told me that they lived in a modest apartment in Coral Gables which is about forty minutes south of Atlantis. Sometimes I spoke with his roomie and gave her study tips. This divorced gentleman spent most of his time working long hours, cooking nutritious meals for his mini-family, renovating their flat, and dreaming of starting his own company.

I was trapped at home. With my intercom set up, I could hear my parents' every move from my room. Between taking care of them and reading everything David Sedaris wrote, I was on the telephone for up to five hours a night, at least three times a week. Mr. Tile and I discussed his business plan, politics, the environment, religion, racism, the state of our society, education, our respective travels throughout the world, music, our favorite books, how to download computer programs, his ancestry, the unfortunate condition my folks were in, our experiences when we lived in Boston, Manhattan, and Washington, D.C, and how lucky we were to have found each other. He helped me through one of the most difficult times in my life. Sometimes simply having someone to talk to is all you really need to make it through the day.

Virtual strangers often comforted me during my parents' illnesses when I least expected it. It was somehow reassuring to know that people were sending me positive thoughts even if I didn't know them well. The medical equipment delivery person called every few weeks to see how I was faring. The UPS guy, nurses from Hospice, the mailman, sanitation workers, handymen, the owner of the landscaping company, and neighbors that I barely spoke to would drop by to say hello and ask if I needed anything. Some of them brought a treat for Muffy and a few prepared goodies to eat. All of them hold a special place in my memory as caring individuals who took a few minutes out of their busy schedules to be kind to someone they hardly knew. Even if you think you are alone in your darkest hours, you never really are. There is always someone looking out for you whether you are mindful of it or not.

## "Wherever I'm planted, I bloom."

Stepping out of my own way in order to serve my parents transformed my perspective on life. I guess being a caretaker makes you reconsider how people treat one another. I've come to the conclusion that it isn't necessary to have an ulterior motive to care about someone. The act of caring should be instinctual, a reflex, a natural impulse. A quote from Marianne Williamson's perpetual calendar reflects how my personal outlook altered during my caretaking responsibilities, "The world changes when we change. The world softens when we soften. The world loves us when we choose to love the world."

Proof that justifies this profound transformative statement will present itself when you become more perceptive and sensitive to others' feelings. Words you read may suddenly jump off the page and smack you between the eyes with enlightenment. Perhaps a prior experience will spring to mind and you'll finally be at peace as to why it happened. Maybe a perfect stranger will utter words that mystically unite your fuzzy thoughts into a single cogent perspective.

After my parents passed, I started attending the opera because of a dream I had of my folks widening their cultural perspectives. It's quite natural for me to chat with individuals seated to my left and right at a performance. However, one evening an elderly lady in front of me suddenly turned around and began conversing. The personable matron spoke of how she didn't want to leave New York but moved to Florida because her husband had dreamed of the warm weather for decades. She concluded her common story with an atypical denouement that astonished me. This wise senior citizen grinned and firmly asserted, "Wherever I'm planted, I bloom." I was stunned by the simplicity of her comment and wholeheartedly thanked her for making me realize that any other way of looking at destiny is pure insanity. Leave it to a grandma to put my life in order with one noble statement.

The last time my dad and I ate lunch together in public was at a former haunt of my parents. The Old Key Lime House restaurant hovers above the Intracoastal Waterway. My father and I sat side by side as we munched on our comfort food.

Every few minutes dad asked *me* if *I* was alright and if *I* needed anything. Those were the only words he spoke towards the end of his life. It still tears the heart right out of me when I think about that final meal we shared. He was full of compassion and only cared for my contentment even though he was just a few months away from gasping for his last breath. That's true benevolence.

I often place adhesive memos on the pages of literature that I'm reading so I can refer to comments that I find significant. Sometimes there are so many colorful reminders of unpretentious yet eloquent truths that I should consider buying stock in the company that manufactures Post-it Notes. One such littered masterpiece is Eckhart Tolle's *The Power of NOW*. Books that challenge my beliefs about the physical and immaterial worlds help me synthesize my experiences. I frequently repeat Mr. Tolle's revelatory words in conversations about caregiving, "Death is a stripping away of all that is not you. The secret of life is to "die before you die" – and find that there is no death." As I work on unraveling that enigma, I find that all my research comes back to the certitude that nothing really matters except love and forgiveness.

# Chapter 15

## "Would you consider changing your career?"

In retrospect I understand my parents did the best they could with the knowledge that was available to them at the time. By observing them I came to realize that fortitude is a strength which needs to be built over a lengthy period just like muscles at the gym. I needed to call upon my inner strength to reconstruct myself after taking care of them.

I started at a Job Fair at The Harriet Himmel Theater in City Place in West Palm Beach. Did I say, "Job Fair?" I don't think so. I've never seen so many stairs at such an insignificant so-called cultural hot spot. There should have been an osteopath and a cardiologist stationed at all of the entrances. People were sweating and huffing and puffing so badly; they prayed that they would live to get to a table which presented them with "an opportunity of a lifetime." I was cheerfully offered employment as a truck driver, a filler of vending machines, a merchant of mattresses, and my personal favorite, a member of the National Guard. There wasn't a single prospect to better yourself unless you had just been released from twenty-five years at Alcatraz and simply wanted something to hold you over until your next heist.

On a more positive note I did learn where the massive City Place parking lot and largest movie theater are located. I now know that I should no longer fantasize about buying a dress at Anthropologie due to the exorbitant prices of tiny pieces of soap. I also found the site of the Teachers' Job Fair at the Convention Center which was scheduled for the following Monday. I looked forward to the possibility that this event might be a cut above the first cluster of so-called "visions of the future." The day's entire ordeal was a worthwhile experience in the long run because it convinced me that I belonged in a classroom. I would die of boredom at any other job.

The highly disappointing Teachers' Job Fair was a typical meat market. I reluctantly completed my first and last year at the charter school. A ridiculously rigorous schedule of paperwork and meetings continued. I wept almost every night because of fatigue, stress, and the fear that I might lose my job if I didn't keep up the pace. I could have endured the insanity if I received a decent salary. At this stage of the game, my hobby was taking out loans. I simply had to get myself into the Palm Beach County Public School System.

A tall, sassy, blonde, first year teacher named Kim was my only ally at work. She had enough testicles for both of us. We quit on the same day shortly after our charter school dismissed the kidlets for summer vacation. Kim also convinced me to accompany her to a Honda showroom near my home. This realistic lady was responsible for persuading me to slowly re-enter the world of the living. After four hours, both of us drove to our respective homes in brand new leased Honda Accords. I was amazed at the technological advancements in cars of our modern age. I damn near cried when I turned on the air conditioner. Good Lord, I could lock the doors and open the trunk and gas cap with a quick click of my fob. I even had a panic button. Heaven help me, I was euphoric listening to music as I eased on down the road. I sat in the carport on quite a few evenings with Muffy on my lap and stared at that new shiny vehicle like it was a freaking Lamborghini.

Kim and I scanned web sites which described local schools in vivid detail. I lowered myself to be interviewed by a panel of nuns at a ritzy private Catholic school on Flagler Drive. There was no way I could have endured their religious intolerance. I figured it was good practice to take a dry run in the hot seat since I hadn't looked for a job in over twenty years. A month before the official school year began, I hit the jackpot. I visited a spotless, safe, and newly constructed public school only seven minutes from my home. I had a conference with the principal and assistant principal and then prayed to receive an offer.

I was intrigued when the savvy administrator called the next day and asked if I'd be interested in changing my career path. She offered me a position not as a fifth grade teacher but as an exceptional student educator because of my Montessori background. Working with children with special needs was an honor that I wished to pursue. She explained how I would have to take an examination in order to become certified in Florida but she was sure I would pass. I accepted the inspiring invitation, studied for twelve hours a day for three weeks, and passed my first nerve shattering computerized test.

A year of red tape began which would have put protocol in Washington, D.C. to shame. I felt as if I was personally responsible for decimating acres of the Amazon rain forest. Shedding tears every night only lasted until February with this job but the paperwork didn't let up. It was a difficult but satisfying year of transition. I knew that I helped third, fourth, and fifth graders who were challenged with special needs build their confidence and academic skills.

Fantastic news arrived during my first week of employment as a Palm Beach County public school employee. A salary scale was instituted and my pay more than doubled. I began developing cahones again. I refinanced my apartment in New York City and paid off all of my debts including the mortgage in Manhattan. The income from my tenants paid for the maintenance and sublet fees for my flat in The Big Apple, my car payment, and a portion of my mortgage in Florida. I could breathe again without worrying about the cost of air.

I became addicted to the home improvement channel on television. I sterilized the house and had the interior and exterior painted in hues that were pleasing to me. I hired a maid to help me twice a month. Furniture was reupholstered and the driveway was resurfaced. New kitchen and master bathroom tray ceilings were installed. I purchased telephones, mattresses, bedding, a headboard, curtains, and three attractive ceiling fans with light fixtures. Landscapers completed sprucing up the grounds and I planted trunk loads of flowering plants and bushes. Area rugs were professionally cleaned. Muffy and I were groomed regularly. I joined a gym around the corner and started working out with a trainer a few times a week. Yoga became my new hobby. The older ladies in Atlantis took me under their wings and invited me to dinner, cocktail parties, and holiday celebrations. Each week I dissected the <u>TGIF</u> section of Friday's <u>Palm Beach Post</u>. I attended plays, concerts, operas, and ballets. I explored museums, historical sites, nature habitats, restaurants, the polo grounds, cinemas, and spas. I found an excellent hairdresser. Golf cart rides with Muff included Gert our elderly neighbor, bird watching and alligator sightings. I discovered that my favorite aspect of Florida is its magical skies and that I simply adored the warmth of the sun.

It is difficult to believe but almost five years have passed since that unforgettable President's Day weekend when I decided to remain in Atlantis for "an undetermined amount of time." These days I am emotionally and physically hearty in Florida. I even received a certificate from my principal for perfect attendance. I figure the powers of the universe bestowed health upon me because I was surrounded by sickness for so long.

My entire existence up until the time my parents died seemed to be a sort of dress rehearsal. I was stunned into recognition of what had really transpired during my decades here on Earth by another extraordinary quotation from Williamson's *A Year of Daily Wisdom*, "Until your knees finally hit the floor, you're just playing at life, and on some level you're scared because you know you're just playing. The moment of surrender is not when life is over. It's when it begins." I surrendered and so did ma and dad. I've heard it said before, "You are forced to grow up when your folks are gone." I am grateful to them because I was compelled to grow up. I know it sounds harsh but on every level, my real life commenced when Claude and Claudine's lives concluded. That's the good ol' tried and true "circle of life."

## "Minimize the crap."

My very being was so altered by my experiences with my parents that I felt like the poster girl for the mythological symbol of resurrection, the phoenix. Claude, Claudine, and Little Claudie were reduced to ashes. We just took different routes and were born again in renovated states. The core of my belief system transformed. Changes occurred in the way I viewed people. My new motto became, "Minimize the crap." I already weeded out my unnecessary possessions. Neighbors often remarked, "Your villa seems so much larger than the others." That's because I cleaned off all of the counter tops and surfaces. I didn't have hundreds of knickknacks on shelves, carpets from the Paleozoic Era, and enough furniture for two houses crowding my home. Minimalism became a way of being.

Old pals who weren't really there for me or for themselves got a line drawn through their names in my address book. I delegated responsibilities and spoke my mind. I kidded incredulous onlookers that my tombstone would read, "She said everything we wanted to say." If I categorized something as bull, I dumped it whether it was attending a villa association meeting, writing a holiday card, or an actual person. Big or small, I fumigated my world.

In return, new and fascinating faces, experiences, and e-mails appeared. The owner of the spa in the Atlantis Mall became a friend. Many parallels in our lives became evident with every conversation. One day she remarked, "Your life seems to be evolving from scars to stars." I was floored by the phrase. She laughed and couldn't believe that I had never heard of that long-standing saying. Insightful Lisa gave me the idea for the title of this book.

Out of the blue, a buddy since infancy decided to purchase a home with her partner in Lake Worth. Maryann is a wise and talented acupuncturist and herbalist. Her treatments tune me up and make me feel like a youngster. A fellow inmate from a Catholic prison known as high school moved to Palm Beach Gardens to marry her long time love. Eleanor and I support one another as we continue to attempt to decipher life's conundrums. Two other dear friends from kindergarten have ties in Florida and visit me regularly.

I began listening to classical music and operas at my home and in my car. I still relish jazz but even my taste in music is not the same. I received a holiday gift certificate from a parent of a Down syndrome student. I raced to Barnes and Noble and purchased a collection of Mozart's concertos and Strauss' waltzes because they simply delight me. That's quite different from saxophone legends, Stan Getz, Gato Barbieri, and Stanley Turrentine.

I now partake in esoteric experiences such as Tarot Card and palm readings and Reiki healing circles. I developed heightened powers of intuition and dream in Technicolor and Dolby Sound. Technology even lent a hand. A pal sent an amazing e-mail which circulated on the Internet. It listed forty-one enlightening principles which were written to celebrate growing older and wiser. Regina Brett of The Plain Dealer of Cleveland, Ohio decided to republish the "most requested column" she'd ever written "as her odometer rolled over to ninety." I took to heart numbers twenty-five through twenty-eight: "What other people think of you is none of your business. Time heals almost everything so give time, time. However good or bad a situation is, the day will come when it will change." My personal favorite is, "Don't take yourself too seriously. No one else does." Once again, a grandmother's sagely advice opened my mind a bit further.

I continued reading self-help books and came across a highly significant movie, Dr. Wayne Dyer's The Shift. He proposed that what a person considers to be a truth in the "morning" of life frequently ends up being a lie in the "afternoon" or "evening." Dr. Dyer explained that key psychological, physiological, and/or spiritual transformations are often heralded by major occurrences such as the loss of a loved one, home, or job; a marriage; a pregnancy; a divorce, separation, or break up; an accident; an illness; something that is perceived as a failure; or a eureka moment. They are all signals that a change in life is imminent. This shift has got to happen no matter who or what are affected or there will be further chaos.

Claude and Claudine ran with the best of them. The problem was they couldn't keep up with the Joneses. Mom and dad never accepted that fact. Pride does come before the fall when people refuse to alter their beliefs and embrace change in spite of how uncomfortable any ongoing adjustments may be. All of our lives are simply a sequence of lessons. Many of them are formidable and have to be reviewed time and time again. I certainly don't want to repeat a term at this university of life on Earth and I pray that the dynamic duo won't be retained.

My counseling sessions enabled me to reconsider how I judged my folks. I came to appreciate the fact that the only way to attain peace of mind is to forgive. My Hospice therapist advised, "Only remember the good times and disregard the rest." In due course, I realized that I am grateful to my parents for teaching me so many important principles even if it was by default on many occasions.

## "Pinch me; I've been happy for three days in a row!"

Of course everyone encounters an occasional turbulent episode during the day or experiences tough weeks, months, or even years. However, the renovation of my belief system allows me the luxury of examining events with a clearer understanding. Therefore, I experience less and shorter periods of being pissed off and offended.

I'm extremely fortunate to be paired up with a diminutive blonde powerhouse at work. Penny is brilliant and spiritually in tune with myself. It is a blessing that we comprehend that there's a reason behind every moment in our lives. Our mutual credence benefits our performance and the manner in which we interact with our intellectually disabled elementary students and their parents or guardians. We understand that all of the children and their families who cross our paths teach us how to improve ourselves.

Long hours at school and in bed at night staring at the ceiling are devoted to devising methods which will guide our pupils through intellectual, emotional, social, and physical obstacles. Every day there is a vast array of rewards we receive from an unexpected hug, a nod of understanding, and a smile of appreciation to that special moment when a child reads or computes independently or with less assistance. We are pleased when there is an increase in diagnostic scores but we're more interested in spotting a twinkle in a child's eye. It's like getting a reconfirming pat on the back from the universe which keeps us on course.

I tried an experiment during my second year as a public school teacher. I felt like an outsider because of my different educational experiences and philosophy. I smiled at everyone and wished them a good day. Now, even the grumpiest teachers and students greet me. I've been accepted as one of them and perhaps I brighten their days. Negative behavior in children and adults is a magnet for unpleasant incidents. As a result, I try to keep a pleasant look on my face and an open heart.

I am consistently grateful for everything in my life because each smidgen of it is there for a specific reason. I envision my bank account whenever I see a homeless person. It wouldn't take very long if I missed a rental payment from Manhattan or a few paychecks for me to be begging on a corner. I frequently imagine myself in another person's shoes or bare feet. That's what my lovely neighbor, Jodine, did.

Holidays don't have much of an effect upon me anymore. They are simply times to relax and extra unhurried moments to work on my writing. I found that some people exhibit genuine concern for me as they rush to complete their gift lists. My first Christmas morning without dad began with a surprise that made me tearful and ever so thankful. I opened the front door for Muffy and followed her as usual. I blinked in disbelief because the trunk of my car had exquisitely wrapped presents on it. I called Muff to come inside and carried my treasures into the living room like an enthusiastic kid.

I munched on peanut brittle as I shredded colorful boxes, tissue paper, and ribbons which contained a bright yellow hooded sweater, stylish earrings, a matching necklace, a darling sun hat, hors d'oeuvre mixes, mouthwatering cookies, a maroon comforter, a magnificent card, and toys for the Muffster. Later that day, Jodine explained how she shopped sporadically throughout the year to make a special collection of surprises for me and that it gave her great joy. This dear woman confided that she admired and loved me. Her statement was the best gift of all. My eyes welled up as I thanked her and hung up the phone. I hardly knew the lady. Her heartfelt expressions kept me cheerful for weeks. I don't really expect presents on my vehicle every Christmas morning but I'm more than pleased that Jodine continues her altruistic tradition.

Friends invite me to visit New York during the holidays, school breaks, and summer vacations. I decline at the present time. I lead a different life now even though I consider my apartment in New York City as an ultimate escape if I need it and a financial ace in the hole. I'm diligent about keeping in touch with comrades via telephone calls, cards, and e-mails. I'm always thrilled to have guests. Patty, my closest and most generous friend since kindergarten, celebrates Easter week with me and usually stays for a spell during business trips. Another dear kindergarten pal, June, visits her brother in Boynton Beach and then drives to Atlantis for a few days. Families from my school in Connecticut call on me throughout the year. Chums from my travels and college days have moved to Florida. Socializing with co-workers was always against my "religion." Now, I occasionally catch a movie and eat dinner with a clever teacher from school.

I'm slowly rebuilding my social life. It's not very difficult to do. I enjoy my own company and never feel alone. That's a benefit of being a Gemini. Going to meals, the cinema, parties, or cultural engagements by myself doesn't bother me at all. In fact, I've travelled solo around the world and prefer it that way. I'm never tied down to anyone and can do what I please. I'm open to whatever destiny brings my way. I let my intuition guide me whether I'm in Miami or Bombay.

Just like a plumber who doesn't seek out sinks on the weekend or a lawyer who doesn't argue cases on Saturday and Sunday, I run for the hills if I see anyone shorter than five feet tall on my days off. Initially, I worked six days a week at my new public school just to keep my head above water. Now, I work my ass off through breaks and lunch and stay late when I have to but rarely bring work home. I give one hundred fifty percent of myself at school and the rest is "me time."

I've become so domestic that I don't recognize myself. Digging in the garden is pure joy. Chores are a pleasure. Painting furniture thrills me. Writing is bliss. At first, I waited for the other shoe to fall. How could I, Claudine Kennedy Seibert, actually be happy? I knew the tide had turned when I expressed my newfound contentment to a supportive confidant, "Pinch me; I've been happy for three days in a row!"

Sure I reminisce about mom and dad. I can't help it when Claude and Claudine want to say, "Hello, we love you. Don't forget us." A while ago I had the pleasure of seeing Tony Bennett perform at The Kravis Center for the Performing Arts in West Palm Beach. He hadn't lost his endearing charm and could still belt out a song like no one else.

I hung my head as tears streamed down my face when Tony crooned one of my mother's favorite tunes, "Stranger in Paradise." My mind ignited when he continued with my beloved ballad, "The Best Is Yet to Come." Eerie, perhaps? I don't think so.

## "I can't believe I'm actually excited to go to Tampa!"

Certain people, activities, reading matter, and innovative information will appear in your life when you are ready to experience a new level of learning and growth. Conversations will crop up which are destined to happen. "Chance" encounters will occur which are preordained. You may pick up a newspaper and read an advertisement for a job or a class that changes your life. Someone can make a playful suggestion that sticks in your mind, takes root, and a lifelong dream may come to fruition such as writing this book. You will emanate higher vibrations. Therefore, you will create and receive more advanced ideas. Signals will most certainly appear that will urge you on to the next stage of development. Signposts and symbols will keep turning up again and again in case you miss them on their first few rounds.

I hadn't taken a vacation in a long time since my parental caretaking responsibilities became more and more demanding. I used to think nothing of flying to Egypt, Barbados, New Mexico, Madrid, or Rome. In Florida I felt privileged to go to the movies or Macy's. One day as I was sitting at my computer preparing lesson plans, "something" told me to check out Dr. Wayne Dyer's itinerary. I had recently viewed his PBS special and all of its reruns concerning his book, Excuses Begone! Lo and behold, he was scheduled to be a keynote speaker at a conference in Tampa, Florida. The three day event of notable thinkers was named, I Can Do It! It was a perfect topic for me to pursue. However, I felt a bit guilty about leaving my students. After a few weeks of deliberation, I decided to take the plunge, lined up an intelligent and trustworthy substitute, and packed my bag.

I couldn't believe that I was actually excited to make the three and one-half hour drive north to Tampa. Talk about a shift in expectations. I got on the Florida Turnpike, turned up the music, and felt freer than a bird that had been released from a sealed cave. Twenty-five minutes into my retreat, I was conversing with a cop. A State Trooper pulled me over for speeding. I had been so thrilled to be driving to a new destination that my right foot took on a life of its own on the accelerator. The stern officer asked for my license and registration. It turned out that I had incorrect registration papers for my car. I was sweating bullets by the time he ran my life through his computer.

Having heard about the ornery reputations of Troopers, I did my best to politely explain that I was a teacher who hadn't taken a vacation in five years. He cut me off and yelled, "Stop! Don't say another word, lady! I haven't had a vacation in five years either. I want you to have the best time you've ever had. Be on your way and don't go more than a couple of miles over 65. Have a safe trip." I thanked him profusely and gaped in disbelief as he sped off down the highway.

I was stunned by his kindheartedness. I had imagined a citation totaling my next paycheck. I speculated about why this happened to me. I deduced that the Trooper had probably saved my life in one way or another because I would always think of him when I was tempted to go over the speed limit. Whew! Any way you look at it I had a good story to tell after my excursion.

I checked into my room at a hotel across the street from the Tampa Convention Center, ordered lunch, gazed out at the bay, and thought how fortunate I was to be there. In fact, if life continued at its present pace, I could officially take my name off the list of certified manic depressives in no time at all.

I received another omen during the first hour of the conference. Louise Hay, author and founder of Hay House publishing and sponsor of the event, made some opening announcements which ended with a mere mention of an upcoming cruise for writers. I felt an actual "pop" inside my head. I truly believe that some sort of seed was planted at that moment. It started to sprout right then and there.

I was thoroughly refreshed and enriched by the end of my hiatus and took off for home. During the next eight months, I felt like a Floridian version of the Oracle at Delphi. Numerous messages came to me that I should write a book about my experiences with my parents. I investigated what was required of a participant in the authors' program at sea. I discovered that a completed manuscript and a book proposal would eventually have to be submitted. I had no idea what a book proposal was. I searched the Internet and found an incredibly interesting, highly detailed, and well-written web site. My first notion was, "How the hell am I going to pull off such a document? It's like a freaking thesis." I decided that I had nothing to lose by e-mailing the professor who wrote the thought-provoking and knowledgeable web pages. This compassionate, erudite, and humorous scholar actually agreed to be my mentor for months on end.

My memories poured out of me day and night. I'd come home from school and the gym and pass out from exhaustion only to get up and write until midnight. I had dreams which guided me what to record. A relative stranger told me that I had an angel on my shoulder that was helping me compose my book. A workshop with two renowned literary agents who provided me with helpful information came to my attention through a close friend in Miami. The UPS guy told me about a resident of Atlantis who recently published a memoir. I contacted the author and she gave me advice about publishing. Two generous buddies knew that I was concerned about financing my literary adventure at sea. They gave me money for my birthday to help pay for my cruise. Even my elderly neighbor told me that I'd be crazy not to participate in a floating seminar for writers because I'd regret it for the rest of my life. Countless instances continually indicated that writing my book and going on the cruise for authors would be beneficial. I recalled Eleanor Roosevelt's quote, "You must do the thing you think you cannot do." So, I did both.

## "I'm definitely going back for more plasma."

Now that we are solidly entrenched in the Age of Technology, e-mails spewing remedies to life's difficulties float freely amongst computers. Many of the same anonymous philosophical essays resurface yearly. Some of the messages are poignant and should be taken to heart. Yet, many of these poetic thoughts conclude with a warning that Beelzebub will pay your loved ones a visit if you don't forward certain announcements to forty-six individuals within twelve seconds. Such threats dampen even the most sacred communications.

I believe that everything happens for a reason so I painstakingly read every single memo that is sent to me via cyberspace. One of the most insightful expositions I received offered an explanation as to why each person we meet should be given serious consideration. Claude and Claudine were an example of a "lifetime relationship." Throughout their lives my folks taught me the power of determination. They never forsook one another or their marriage for more than half a century. Today, couples divorce if one of them neglects to turn on the coffee maker in the morning.

My godmother's eldest daughter presciently passed on the piece, <u>People Come into Your Life for a Reason, a Season, or a Lifetime</u>, three months before dad died. The unknown author is a modern day sage who spoke to my soul. He/She wrote: "… When someone is in your life for a reason, it is usually to meet a need you have expressed. They have come to assist you through a difficulty, to provide you with guidance and support, and to aid you physically, emotionally, or spiritually. They may seem like a godsend and they are. They are there for the reason you need them to be. Then, without any wrongdoing on your part or at an inconvenient time, this person will say or do something to bring the relationship to an end. Sometimes they die. Sometimes they walk away. Sometimes they act up and force you to take a stand. What we must realize is that our need has been met; our desire fulfilled; their work is done. The prayer you sent up has been answered and now it is time to move on with your life.

Some people come into your life for a season because your turn has come to share, grow, or learn. They bring you an experience of peace or make you laugh. They may teach you something you have never done. They usually give you an unbelievable amount of joy. Believe it. It is real but only for a season.

Lifetime relationships teach you lifetime lessons, ideas you must build upon in order to have a solid emotional foundation. Your job is to accept the lesson; love the person; and put what you have learned to use in all other relationships and areas of your life.

It is said that love is blind but friendship is clairvoyant."

I've been an elementary school teacher for more than two decades. It's become a habit to share what I perceive to be astute perceptions or anything I classify as valuable information. I've learned that scientists estimate the universe exploded into being between twelve and fifteen billion years ago. Research suggests that all matter, space, and time began at that cataclysmic moment. It is also well documented that everything in the universe is composed of four elements: liquid, solid, gas, and plasma. Microsoft Encarta Dictionary defines plasma as "… a hot gas made up of ions and electrons that is found in the Sun and stars."

I was a Montessori teacher for twenty-five years. The Montessori philosophy of education utilizes stories based on fact to relate a variety of lessons to pupils. I used to communicate to my students that human beings are a combination of all four elements. I explained that blood is a liquid; bone is a solid; and gas is in the lungs. Stardust from exploding stars called supernovas makes up some of the necessary building blocks of life such as oxygen and carbon. Therefore, we are comprised of plasma just like stars. When anything dies, it doesn't really come to an end. It merely changes form like a supernova. Consider the trees in the forests that eventually fall and ultimately nurture the soil. Coal is made from trees that were compressed in the Earth for millions of years. Allow that coal to remain in the ground for a few more million years and diamonds appear.

I guess that's why I turned Claude and Claudine into stars when they died. I figured I could keep track of them for a while. I don't know much about astronomy but I've read that constellations change their positions throughout the year. When I could no longer locate mom and dad in the night sky, I simply told myself they were vacationing in an exclusive part of the Southern Hemisphere.

My parents faced the highs and lows that life offered and were often wounded by their experiences. They were like steadfast soldiers, who after a respite with the medics, carried on with their missions. Every existence is merely a succession of demanding lessons which have to be repeated until the concepts are thoroughly understood and practiced. I certainly learned a lot under my family's tutelage and wholeheartedly love them and thank them for the knowledge they bestowed upon me. Claude and Claudine guided me to understand that I always have a choice be it stardust to stardust or scars to stars. Either way, I'm definitely going back for more plasma. The bottom line is that everyone who I cared about in my family has passed. I have no kids and I married a poodle. I'm one of the happiest people I know.

My folks' memorable photograph displayed at their funerals.